great food finds

CAPE COD

Delicious Food from
the **Region's Top Eateries**

John F. Carafoli
Featuring photography from
Francine Zaslow and **Manx Taiki Magyar**

Globe Pequot

Guilford, Connecticut

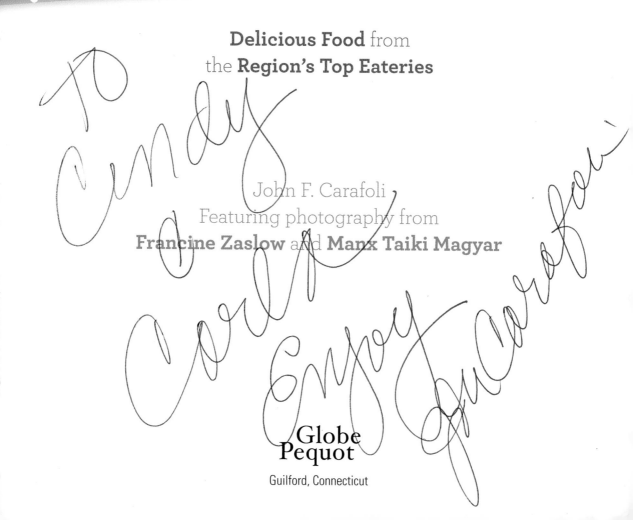

Globe
Pequot

An imprint of The Rowman & Littlefield Publishing Group, Inc.
4501 Forbes Blvd., Ste. 200
Lanham, MD 20706
www.rowman.com

Distributed by NATIONAL BOOK NETWORK

British Library Cataloguing in Publication Information Available

Library of Congress Cataloging-in-Publication Data available

ISBN 978-1-4930-2811-5 (paperback)
ISBN 978-1-4930-2816-0 (e-book)

♾™ The paper used in this publication meets the minimum requirements of American National Standard for Information Sciences—Permanence of Paper for Printed Library Materials, ANSI/NISO Z39.48-1992.

Restaurants and chefs often come and go, and menus are ever-changing. We recommend you call ahead to obtain current information before visiting any of the establishments in this book.

For John. He sings, and I cook.

CONTENTS

INTRODUCTION

Cape Cod is more than just fun clam shacks offering fried clams and clam chowder. Yes, there are many good ones, but today there is so much more. There is a new energy in the restaurant and food world on the Cape. Chefs with families are moving here and starting their own restaurants. You can now find Italian, Brazilian, Mexican, Peruvian and French restaurants, but there is always that touch of Cape Cod cultural DNA in each restaurant, fresh and local. Chefs are reinventing some of the old New England classics. For example, one chef has updated the traditional clam chowder by replacing white potatoes with sweet potatoes. Another adds lobster to the classic Benedict. Try a new twist on the classic cheesecake, with lavender and goat cheese.

Some of the chefs' dishes included in this book may seem complicated at first, like Twenty-Eight Atlantic Chef James Hackney's Caramelized Scallops. This is really a number of recipes within one. Instead of making the entire recipe, however, you could make the pea puree for one dish, or use his gnocchi recipe for a first course with a light marinara sauce or just a sage butter.

This book follows the same road a visitor would take when visiting the Cape. Everyone goes over the Sagamore or Bourne Bridge and travels down Route 6 or turns off to Route 28 or Route 6A. The book does the same thing. It winds through the fifteen towns and their respective villages to explore each town and its environment through a new lens. I talked to chefs about the food they serve and where they get their produce and products. I found many new small, out-of-the-way places and tasted many of the products the local cottage industries have to offer like tasty shrubs, homemade granola, jams and jellies, and the best place for a good donut. I also located new restaurants like Water Street Kitchen in Woods Hole and Viera in Harwich.

I have tried to make this more than just a cookbook by adding my own remembrances, thoughts, and experiences about the Cape as it was in the past and is today. This is my Cape Cod, the place where I have a picnic after a day at the beach and celebrate special occasions with friends and family with dinner at home or at one of these fine restaurants. Join me for this food journey along the Cape—it will be fun, with a variety of fresh, local delicious food!

UPPER CAPE

Amie Bakery

Amie likes to think of her kitchen as the "town's kitchen," and feels the best place to connect with people is around a table. The one thing she enjoys more than baking for neighbors is spending time with them.

"French toast is such a special treat," says Amie, "and when my mom made it she soaked two pieces of white bread in egg and milk, cooked it in a buttered frying pan, and topped it with maple syrup. She never added any vanilla or spices. This is not my mother's French toast. With the addition of almond cream (frangipane), our French Toast is a nod to my mother's but combines all the flavors of what my palate dreams of when I think about traditional pastries from years gone by."

3 Wianno Avenue, Osterville, MA 02655, (508) 428-1005, amiebakerycc.com

FRENCH TOAST

(Serves 4)

FOR THE BATTER:

¼ cup heavy cream

1 cup milk

½ cup sugar

Zest of 1 orange

1 tablespoon vanilla extract

2 eggs

1 teaspoon cardamom

FOR THE ALMOND CREAM (FRANGIPANE):

7 ounces almond paste

½ cup sugar

4 eggs

7 ounces butter

2 teaspoon vanilla extract

½ cup all-purpose flour

½ teaspoon baking powder

FOR THE TOAST:

1 pound loaf of bread, preferably brioche, sliced and cubed (day old/stale bread is good, but if you don't have time use fresh)

1–1½ cups berries (raspberries, blackberries, blueberries, or any berries you prefer)

To make the batter: In a large bowl, whisk together heavy cream, milk, sugar, orange zest, vanilla, eggs, and cardamom. Add the bread to the batter and allow it to soak while you make the frangipane.

To make the almond cream (frangipane): Beat together the almond paste, sugar, and one egg until smooth. Beat in butter and vanilla.

Beat in the remaining 3 eggs, one at a time, until smooth, scraping the bowl and paddle. Combine flour and baking powder and add to the mixture. Mix on low speed until absorbed.

To assemble: Create a layer of the soaked bread on the bottom of a buttered four baking cups or ramekin. Pipe or spread about a ¼ cup of almond cream on top. Sprinkle berries on top. Add a second layer of the soaked bread. Garnish with a dollop of almond cream and a berry on top.

Bake at 350°F for 25–35 minutes until golden brown.

Sprinkle finished toasts with confectioners' sugar and serve with maple syrup.

Note: You can store any extra almond cream in the refrigerator for up to two weeks. Or you can use it as the base of a fruit tarte.

All Cape Cook's Supply

Pam and Tom Cooney started this business over 18 years ago. This amazing store caters to restaurateurs, professional chefs, and serious amateur cooks. The merchandise is stuck in every corner of the store. Everything from hundreds of metal cookie-cutter shapes, to large commercial strainers, to dozens of teapots and peppermills, and all manner of baking pans, knives, glassware, electric appliances, cast iron, bottles and jars, pastry boards, and, believe me, much more! If Pam does not have it, she will get it for you. It is fun explore the shop—you will always find things you don't need!

237 Main Street, Hyannis, MA 02601, (508) 790-8908

Añejo Mexican Bistro & Tequila Bar

Since August 2010, Añejo has been a bustling establishment on Main Street in Falmouth, a surprising taste of Mexico in this fairly traditional town. The owners are Jesse Kersey and Jamie Surprenant. Jesse grew up in the San Francisco area, and Jamie was raised on Cape Cod and worked in his family's restaurant for two decades. He is also a co-owner of the successful Five Bays Bistro in Osterville.

The bar has over sixty-five different brands of tequila to choose from, ranging from Bianco (silver) and Reposado (aged), to the Añejo (extra-aged). The menu runs the gamut. Choose from the freshly made tableside guacamole in an authentic molcajete served with plenty of fresh, crisp tortillas to house specials like the recipe shown here.

188 Main Street, Falmouth, MA 02540, (508) 388-7631, anejomexicanbistro.com

GUACAMOLE
(Serves 4)

4 Hass ripe avocados, halved,
  pitted, and peeled
½ white sweet onion, peeled and
  finely chopped
½ bunch fresh cilantro, finely
  chopped
1 jalapeño, stemmed, seeded,
  and finely chopped
2 tablespoons fresh lime juice
  (from 1 lime)
Cotija cheese, for garnish

Smash avocados to desired consistency. Add remaining ingredients and mix well. Transfer to a serving bowl and press a sheet of plastic wrap directly against the surface of the guacamole until ready to serve. Remove plastic wrap and sprinkle with cotija cheese before serving.

Serve with tortilla chips and a margarita.

PESCADO ENCORNFLECADO

(Serves 6)

FOR THE SALSA VERDE:

1 pound (11–12) fresh tomatillos, husked, washed, and cut into chunks

2 cups chicken broth

2 jalapeños or 3 serrano chiles, stemmed, cut in half, and seeded

1 tablespoon vegetable oil

1 small yellow onion, peeled and chopped

1 garlic clove, peeled and chopped

2 tablespoons chopped fresh cilantro

Salt to taste

FOR THE RICE:

2 cups water

1 cup long-grain Basmati rice

1 tablespoon butter

FOR THE COD:

½ cup all-purpose flour

1 teaspoon salt

2 large eggs

3 tablespoons water

6 cups crushed cornflakes

6 (5–6 ounce) skinless cod fillets, about ¾-inch thick

¼ cup corn oil, more if needed, for each fillet

For the salsa verde: Place tomatillos, chicken broth, and chiles in a saucepan and bring to a boil. Cook until vegetables are fairly soft, about 5 to 10 minutes. Meanwhile, heat the oil in a sauté pan and add the onion. Cook, stirring occasionally, until softened, about 5 minutes. Add the garlic and cook 1 minute more. Stir in the boiled tomatillos and chiles and remove from heat. Transfer to a food processor, along with the cilantro and salt to taste. Blend until smooth. Set aside.

For the rice: Bring water to boil in a medium-size saucepan with a lid. Stir in the rice and butter. Cover the pan, reduce heat to low, and simmer until rice is tender and water is absorbed, about 20 minutes. Set aside and keep warm.

For the cod: Preheat oven to 350°F. Set up three shallow dishes to make a breading station. Place the flour in the first dish and mix in ½ teaspoon salt. Combine the eggs, water, and ½ teaspoon salt in the second dish and beat with a fork until well blended. Place the cornflakes in the third dish. Dredge each fillet in flour, shaking off any excess; turn the fish in the beaten egg; and then transfer the fish to the cornflakes, pressing firmly to thoroughly coat on all sides. Place coated fillets on a plate in a single layer without touching, as they are breaded. Heat the oil in a sauté pan and lightly brown each fillet. Transfer to a baking sheet and bake until just cooked through, about 8 minutes.

For the corn: Preheat the grill to medium-high and grill the corn, turning occasionally, until lightly charred, about 8 to 10 minutes. Transfer to a platter. Quickly spread the corn with mayonnaise and then roll in the cheese. Sprinkle a small amount of cayenne or chili powder on each ear.

To assemble the dish: At serving time, stir the cilantro, lime juice, and zest into the rice. Mound some rice on each dinner plate and arrange fish fillets on top. Spoon salsa verde over the fish. Complete each plate with an ear of corn, a sprinkle of cotija cheese, and a lime wedge.

FOR THE CORN:
6 ears fresh corn, shucked and silks removed
6 tablespoons mayonnaise
¾ teaspoon cayenne pepper or chili powder
4–6 tablespoons finely shredded cotija or Parmesan cheese

TO ASSEMBLE THE DISH:
½ cup chopped fresh cilantro
2 tablespoons fresh lime juice (from 1 lime)
1 teaspoon grated lime zest
1 cup cotija cheese, grated
1–2 limes, cut into wedges

Belfry Inn & Bistro

Between 1995 and 2003, Christopher Wilson purchased and renovated three run-down buildings on Jarves Street in the heart of the village of Sandwich. These three buildings—a Victorian building known as "the Painted Lady," a deconsecrated Roman Catholic Church, and a federal-style building that once housed the company that built the Cape Cod Canal—were renovated and transformed into the Belfry Inn & Bistro.

The Bistro is in the church, which is now known as the Abbey. Wilson used ingenuity and imagination as he salvaged and reused as much of the original church as possible. The one-time confessional is now the wine cellar, and many of the pews have been put to different uses. Some became the bar, some were used as paneling for the walls, and some became beds. Still in their original homes, however, are most of the stained-glass windows, and the grand fireplace is now the focal point of the main dining room.

The food served in this architectural marvel is some of the best you will find on the Upper Cape. The menu is varied, with tasting plates, lighter fare, and gluten-free offerings. You can have Cape Littlenecks in chowder or baked and stuffed. For entrees there's Dayboat Chatham Codfish, Seared Local Sea Scallops, or Atlantic Halibut.

You can eat at the bar, dine in the main room, or, in warmer weather, sit outside on the patio. There's a wine tasting every Wednesday evening, and the Bistro does catering for special events and weddings. Treat yourself to a dining experience here. The combination of extraordinary surroundings and wonderful food is heavenly.

8 Jarves Street, Sandwich, MA 02563, (508) 888-8550, belfryinn.com

Bleu

Mashpee Commons is an open-air shopping mall created to look like a New England town center. On the way to New Seabury and Falmouth, it's a good place to stop for a little shopping, an ice cream cone, or a lovely French meal. Chef Frederick Feufeu, a native of the Loire Valley, went to the celebrated Les Sorbets School in Brittany. He spent some time in Paris and London and eventually found himself working at some of the best restaurants in New York City, including the Rainbow Room and the Brasserie Pascal.

After marriage and children, Chef Feufeu and his wife decided to make a change. He had always thought of having his own restaurant, and because he had a connection to Cape Cod, it seemed a likely place to do it.

Chef Feufeu opened his bistro in 2003, and his fine cooking has become a year-round staple in the Mashpee area. The comfortable room with its understated decor complements his French style of cooking. The waitstaff is friendly, attentive, and knowledgeable. In warmer months there is outdoor seating, but during the winter months, it is a cozy comfortable place for a quiet French dinner for any occasion. You'll find Chef Feufeu's classic French touch in dishes like the Escargot de Bourgogne Farcis and the French Onion Soup. There is plenty of fresh fish prepared in a variety of different ways on the menu, along with steaks, lamb, and chicken. On special days of the week, try the special three-course prix fixe menu.

10 Market Street, Mashpee Commons, Mashpee, MA 02649, (508) 539-7907, bleurestaurant.com

ESCARGOTS WITH GARLIC BUTTER

(Serves 6)

FOR THE GARLIC BUTTER:

2 cups (1 pound) unsalted butter, softened

1 cup chopped fresh curly parsley

¼ cup Pernod

10 garlic cloves, minced

2 tablespoons chopped fresh thyme

1 teaspoon fine sea salt

1 (16-ounce) can escargots, rinsed and drained well, with shells if desired

Crusty French bread, for serving

For the garlic butter: Combine the butter, parsley, Pernod, garlic, thyme, and salt in a bowl and mix until thoroughly blended. Garlic butter can be prepared ahead; cover and refrigerate. Bring to room temperature before using.

To assemble the dish: Preheat oven to 400°F. Bring a pot of water to boil. Add the escargots, cook 2 minutes, then drain and rinse with cold water to stop the cooking. If using shells, stuff each shell generously with garlic butter, add an escargot, top with more butter, and place in a gratin dish. (Unbaked escargots can be refrigerated, tightly covered, for up to 1 week.) Bake until hot and bubbly, about 7 minutes. Serve immediately with crusty French bread.

ONION SOUP GRATINÉE

(Serves 6)

¼ cup olive oil
1 tablespoon unsalted butter
4 large onions, peeled and sliced
    ¼ inch thick
2 cups dry red wine
2–3 sprigs fresh thyme
1 garlic clove, minced
1 bay leaf
6 cups chicken stock
2 cups rich beef stock

12 stale baguette slices
2 cups (16 ounces) grated
    Gruyère cheese

Heat the oil and butter together in a large heavy pot over medium heat. Turn the heat up to medium-high and then add the onions and sauté, stirring and turning frequently, until they are dark brown and very soft, about 30 minutes. Turn the heat to high and add the wine, thyme, garlic, and bay leaf. Cook, scraping up any browned bits stuck to the pan, until wine has reduced by half, about 10 minutes. Add the chicken and beef stocks and bring to a boil. Adjust heat to a simmer and cook about 45 minutes.

Preheat broiler or oven to 400°F. Arrange six individual soup crocks or ovenproof bowls on a sturdy baking sheet. Remove thyme sprigs and bay leaf and ladle the soup into the bowls. Fit two baguette slices on top of each and cover with a generous amount of cheese. Bake until cheese melts to a crispy brown, about 3 minutes.

The Brown Jug

Like most of the buildings in Sandwich, the two buildings that Michael Johnston owns have had many incarnations. In the 1920s the building on Main Street was a grocery store and then a diner. The building on Jarves Street dates back to 1873, when it was a shoe and boot store and in later years a meeting hall for Civil War veterans. Sometime after that it became a dry goods store called Butner's. But now the corner of Main and Jarves is home to The Brown Jug.

The Brown Jug opened on Main Street in the fall of 2003, offering specialty foods, ceramics, and linens from around the world. The wine room opened the following spring around the corner on Jarves Street, and by 2009 The Brown Jug had expanded to include a café as well as a cappuccino and latte bar. It is one of the best places on the Cape to buy wonderful cheeses and wines, enjoy a cocktail or a glass of wine with lunch on the outdoor patio, or even have a party catered.

Johnston traveled widely before settling down in Sandwich. "My mother was in the restaurant business, so I grew up with it," he says. "I went to school in England and then in Canada and worked in the food, beverage, and hospitality business. I worked at the Four Seasons hotel in Boston, then bought a home here in Sandwich." Michael emphasizes the importance of good communication with his patrons. "Customers will come in and tell me that they are having a party or special gathering for twenty people and want something special for the occasion. I first ask for a few guidelines, such as how many people, what is the price line, what are you comfortable with. I am totally comfortable with their needs. Then the fun begins for me! I do best when my customers let me create something within their needs."

155 Main Street, Sandwich, MA 02563, (508) 888-4669, thebrownjug.com, Owner: Michael Johnston

The Chart Room

The Chart Room is a seasonal restaurant with rustic Cape Cod charm. It is casual and fun and has great fresh seafood. It is open for lunch or dinner, and you can choose to eat outside on the lawn or inside at either the long bar or an individual table. All seats have a great view of the harbor. Some evenings have lively entertainment, but almost all evenings have beautiful, breathtaking sunsets.

David Jarvis runs the front of the house and the bar while Chef Tom Gordon runs the kitchen. They have been business partners for over forty years. Both are native New Englanders.

"This business started with my parents and their friends Gordon Swanson—Swannie as we called him—and his wife," says Jarvis. Tom Gordon started in the kitchen as a dishwasher under Swannie and says, "The biggest sellers on our menu are the baked stuffed lobsters, the lobster salad sandwich, and the swordfish."

The interior of the restaurant is covered with memorabilia and history. Jarvis points to various signs on the walls of the restaurant. "People actually bring me things to pin up. Over there is a sign from Swift's Market, in Osterville; another sign was given to us by a gentleman who retired his boat and wanted the sign to be hung here. There have been years and years of people bringing me signs to put up."

1 Shipyard Lane, Cataumet, MA 02534, (508) 563-5350, chartroomcataumet.com

STEAMED MUSSELS

(Serves 4)

½ cup olive oil
¼ cup chopped garlic
2–3 sprigs fresh thyme
1–2 bay leaves
4 pounds mussels, scrubbed and
  beards removed
1 cup white wine
¼ cup water
Parsley for garnish

Combine the olive oil, garlic, thyme, and bay leaves in a large Dutch oven or other pot with a lid. Sauté over medium heat 5 minutes, stirring occasionally; be careful not to burn the garlic. Add the mussels and raise the heat to high; add the wine and water and mix well. Cover and cook, shaking the pot a few times, until the mussels open, about 10 minutes. Discard any mussels that do not open. Divide mussels, along with the cooking liquid, among 4 bowls and garnish with parsley.

BAKED STUFFED LOBSTER

(Serves 2)

FOR THE BREAD CRUMBS:
1–1½ cups fine dry bread crumbs
¼ teaspoon garlic powder
¼ teaspoon onion powder
¼ teaspoon dried parsley flakes
¼ teaspoon paprika
¼ teaspoon white pepper
3–4 tablespoons unsalted butter,
  melted
2 (1½–pound) lobsters, split and
  thoroughly cleaned
10–12 ounces freshly cooked
  lobster meat
½ cup unsalted butter, melted

For the bread crumbs: Place bread crumbs in a bowl and add the spices; mix well. Add just enough melted butter to evenly moisten; set aside.

To assemble the dish: Preheat oven to 450°F. Place the lobsters cut side up on a baking sheet and loosely stuff cavities with lobster meat. Drizzle the meat with melted butter, top with seasoned bread crumbs, and cover each stuffed cavity with a small piece of foil to prevent burning. Bake until golden brown, about 15 to 20 minutes.

Ben & Bill's Chocolate Emporium

Every time I go to Falmouth, it is a tradition for me to stop in this old-fashioned Emporium for two chocolate almond clusters. I also check out the special creative ice creams and frozen gelatos.

Paul and Mary Trahan started making handmade candies and chocolates in Vineyard Haven, MA, in 1956. Trahan's Candies turned into a much larger operation with many locations from Palm Beach, Florida, to Bar Harbor, Maine. Each location makes its own flavors. In the summer the Falmouth shop makes over 40 different flavors and gelatos.

Once when I was there, they had made Lobster Ice Cream––yes, made with real lobster meat. The last time I was there one of their biggest sellers was the "KGB."

This is a success story of two people in New England selling chocolates, growing their operation over the years into a thriving family business. In 1988 it was sold to their nephews, Benjamin and William Coggins, and renamed Ben & Bill's. The Falmouth store is managed and run by Jeannette Michaud and Erin Kotchian.

209 Main Street, Falmouth, MA 02540, (508) 548-7878, Benandbills.Com

Crow Farm

After a long winter, Crow Farm is one of those special places one looks forward to opening in May. At the beginning of the month, you'll find jams, jellies, and local honey. But by the end of the month, when it's time to plant on Cape Cod, you'll find enough for your own instant garden. Choose from tomatoes, peas, cucumbers, eggplant, a variety of peppers (regular and hot), squashes, and herbs that were started months ago in Crow Farm's greenhouses. As the summer season builds, so does the bounty in this small white building, nestled by the side of the road in East Sandwich. It starts with different lettuces and fresh flowers in June and continues into July with juicy yellow and white peaches and corn. Crow Farm is one of the few farms on the Cape that still grows and sells local corn. In late summer there are crisp varieties of apples. When fall hits, it's time to fill the gardens and pathways with abundantly colored mums and pumpkins. And toward Christmas you can pick up your tree, a wreath, or a lovely poinsettia plant.

In addition to this bounty of fruits, vegetables, and flowers there's Ellen Crowell's baked goods. Homemade breads and pies made with homegrown fruits are popular with locals and tourists. And the fact that all this happens on a farm that has been owned by the same family for almost one hundred years seems to add to the flavor. Crow Farm began in 1916 when brothers David and Lincoln Crowell purchased forty acres of land. Paul Crowell is the third generation to work the farm, and his son Jason will be the fourth. Stop by to experience this Cape Cod treasure.

192 Route 6A, East Sandwich, MA 02563, (508) 888-0690

ELLEN CROWELL'S BLUEBERRY BREAD

(Serves 6–8)

1 cup plus 2 tablespoons sugar,
  divided
½ cup (4 ounces) unsalted butter,
  slightly softened
2 eggs
1 ½ teaspoons vanilla extract
2 cups all-purpose flour
2 teaspoons baking powder
½ teaspoon salt
½ cup milk
2 ½ cups fresh blueberries,
  washed, dried, and
  picked over

Preheat oven to 375°F.

Butter an 8½ X 4–inch loaf pan and set aside. Combine 1 cup sugar and the butter in a large mixing bowl and beat with an electric mixer until light and fluffy. Add the eggs, one at a time, beating well after each addition. Add the vanilla and mix well.

Combine the flour, baking powder, and salt in another bowl. Add the dry ingredients to the batter in three additions, alternating with the milk.

Gently fold in the blueberries and pour the batter into the prepared pan. Sprinkle the remaining 2 tablespoons sugar over the batter and bake until a toothpick inserted in the center comes out clean, 50 to 60 minutes. Cool in a pan for 10 minutes and turn out on a rack to cool completely. Wrap and store at room temperature or refrigerate.

E&T Farms

Two streets over from where I live in West Barnstable is a place I can buy hydroponic (plants grown in water) salad greens, micro greens, beautiful golden honey, and shrimp year round!

It is a family-owned business run by Edward and Betty Osmun. They started the farm 15 years ago. I asked Ed how he got started with this farm: "It was my passion and just something I wanted to do!"

For several years Ed farmed tilapia and bass and used the fish water for fertilizing the hydroponic lettuces. He went on to say, "But I cannot use the shrimp water because it is salt water from Cape Cod Bay." Every 6 months Ed harvests his shrimp. They run about 20 count per pound.

85 Lombard Avenue, West Barnstable, MA 02668, (508) 362-8370, eandtfarminc.com

STIR-FRIED WHOLE SHRIMP

(Serves 4)

We rarely find whole shrimp with heads in our local fish markets. Here is a chance to have a fully unique experience. Most of the shrimp is edible. Pull the meat from the head and suck the juices from the inside—it is delicious!

2 pounds whole, heads-on
    shrimp
3 tablespoons sesame oil for
    stir-frying
2 cups vegetables for stir-frying
    (broccoli, onions, mushrooms,
    bean sprouts, or water
    chestnuts)
1 teaspoon cornstarch mixed
    with ¼ cup water
½ cup sauce for stir-frying (a
    spicy Szechuan sauce, a
    tangy sweet and sour sauce,
    or a sweet teriyaki sauce)
4 cups cooked rice or noodles
1 tablespoon salt

Pour the sesame oil into the wok or large nonstick skillet. Heat the oil over high heat. Add the shrimp and quickly sauté for three minutes, or until the shells turn pink. Add vegetables and sauté the mixture for two minutes; the vegetables should be tender but not soft. Add cornstarch slurry to the chosen sauce and quickly stir into the shrimp and vegetables mixture until sauce thickens, 1-2 minutes. Serve the stir-fried shrimp and vegetables hot over rice or noodles. Allow the diners to peel and eat the shrimp themselves and don't forget what is in the head!

Ella's Wood Burning Oven Restaurant

Marc and Bree Swierkowski own and operate Ella's Wood Burning Oven in Wareham, just on the boarder of Buzzardsd Bay and Wareham

From the street the restaurant looks unassuming, but inside the atmosphere is comfortable and casual. Marc is a wonderful chef, and his food never disappoints. I tried one of the dishes we had discussed, the Buttermilk Fried Chicken. Delicious.

I asked Marc about what inspires him. "When I have an opportunity to travel to a new region, I am inspired by the culture and local chefs. Many times there's a new ingredient that I haven't used before, or not for a very long time, that is available through a purveyor or a farmers' market," he says. "As this industry grows, we as chefs need to grow and run with the trends but still keep the integrity of the dish. With so many ingredients and so many chefs, the thing that I believe distinguishes us is quality, and knowing the authentic techniques of cooking." Chef Swierkowski's food is some of the best on the Upper Cape.

3136 Cranberry HWY, East Wareham MA 02538, (508) 759-3600

FRESH LITTLENECK CLAM CHOWDER

(Serves 4–6)

8 tablespoons (4 ounces)
   unsalted butter, divided
3 slices thick-cut bacon, diced
½ cup chopped onions
⅓ cup chopped celery
2 bay leaves
2 cups sea clam juice
½ cup peeled and grated russet
   potato
¼ cup peeled and grated sweet
   potato
1 cup heavy cream
12–16 littleneck clams, shells
   scrubbed of sand
1 (6-ounce) sweet potato, peeled
   and diced
1 tablespoon chopped fresh
   thyme
8 dashes Tabasco sauce
Salt and pepper to taste

Combine 4 tablespoons butter and the bacon in a heavy-bottomed 4-quart pot over medium-low heat. Cook until the butter is melted and the bacon is crisp, stirring often.

Raise the heat to medium-high and add the onions, celery, and bay leaves; sauté until onion is translucent, about 5 minutes.

Add the clam juice and bring to a boil. Adjust the heat and simmer for 10 minutes to blend flavors.

Add the grated potatoes, stirring constantly, until potatoes are softened and chowder starts to thicken, about 8 to 10 minutes.

Remove the pan from the heat, take out the bay leaves, and use an immersion blender to puree the chowder base.

Return the chowder to the pot. Stir in the cream and return the pot to medium-high heat. Bring to a boil, stirring often.

Add the clams, diced sweet potato, remaining 4 tablespoons butter, thyme, and Tabasco; return to a simmer and cook, stirring often, just until clams open and potatoes are tender. Remove from heat and season with salt and pepper to taste.

To serve, divide the opened clams among soup bowls, and ladle the chowder over them.

BUTTERMILK FRIED CHICKEN

(Serves 4–6)

FOR THE BRINE:

1 gallon water
1 cup kosher salt
½ cup sugar
8 bay leaves
2 cinnamon sticks
2 tablespoons whole black
　　peppercorns
5 allspice berries
5 whole cloves
2½ pounds all natural chicken,
　　preferably 2 breasts,
　　2 drumsticks, and 2 thighs

FOR THE FRIED CHICKEN:

2 cups all-purpose flour
2 tablespoons onion powder
2 tablespoons garlic powder
2 tablespoons smoked paprika
1 teaspoon cayenne pepper
1 tablespoon kosher salt
2 teaspoons cracked black
　　pepper
2 cups buttermilk
Vegetable, canola, or peanut oil
　　for frying

TO GARNISH:

¼ cup honey
Coarse sea salt

For the brine: Combine brine ingredients in a large pot over high heat, stirring to dissolve the salt and sugar. Bring to a boil, then adjust the heat to a simmer and cook 5 minutes. Remove from heat and chill thoroughly. Place chicken in the brine; refrigerate for 12 to 24 hours.

For the fried chicken: Combine the flour, onion powder, garlic powder, paprika, cayenne, salt, and cracked pepper in a large shallow bowl and mix well. Place the buttermilk in another shallow bowl and set aside. Fill a Dutch oven or large cast iron skillet halfway with oil and place over medium-high heat. Attach a candy thermometer to the pan and heat the oil to 350°F.

While the oil is heating, coat the chicken: Working with one piece at a time, roll the chicken in the flour mixture, shaking off any excess, then dip in buttermilk to coat completely. Return the chicken to the flour, rolling and turning to make sure there are no bare spots. Leave the chicken in the flour for a few minutes, then roll it to coat again. Transfer the pieces to a wire rack as they are done, making sure coated pieces do not touch.

Carefully add the chicken to the hot oil and fry for 10 to 13 minutes, until the internal temperature of a thigh reaches 155°F on an instant-read thermometer. Drain the cooked chicken on paper towels, then transfer to a clean wire rack to rest in a warm place for 5 minutes before serving. (This will allow the chicken to reach its proper serving temperature.) If the chicken gets cold, reheat in a 375°F oven.

To assemble the dish: Place a large spoonful of watermelon salad on each plate. Arrange the fried chicken beside it and garnish the chicken with a drizzle of honey and a sprinkle of salt. Serve immediately.

For the watermelon salad: Combine the salad ingredients in a bowl and toss gently to combine. Can be prepared a day ahead; cover and refrigerate until serving.

FOR THE WATERMELON SALAD:

¼ seedless watermelon, rind removed and flesh cut in cubes

1½ cups fresh corn kernels (from 3 ears sweet corn)

1 pint cherry tomatoes, washed, dried, and quartered

1 small red onion, peeled and diced

2 jalapeños, stemmed, seeded, and diced

2 limes, zested and juiced

¼ cup thinly sliced fresh mint leaves

¼ cup honey

¼ cup extra-virgin olive oil

The Bourne Scallop Festival

The Scallop Festival, now in its forty-fourth year, originated
with a group of local fishermen who wanted to celebrate
their catch. Over the years it's been held in several different
locations, including a huge tent on Main Street in Bourne, near
the train station on the scenic Cape Cod Canal and Railroad
Bridge (the second-largest lift bridge in the United States).
Due to the large crowds it attracts, the Festival outgrew its
quaint original setting and is now held at the Cape Cod Fair
Grounds, 1220 Nathan Ellis Hwy Rt. 151 East Falmouth.

Held in September (the third weekend after Labor Day,
Friday through Sunday), the festival is one of the biggest
events on Cape Cod. Each year over fifty thousand people
show up to feast on sea scallops, herb-roasted chicken, and
fish and chips. There is also a large food court with a variety
of other foods and wine and beer. The festival includes an arts
and craft show, a huge midway of rides and games for the kids,
and live entertainment by local musicians in the main tent.
It is a family-oriented event put on by the Cape Cod Canal
Region Chamber of Commerce.

Marie Oliva, president and CEO of the chamber, says,
"This isn't your average festival. The community has a big

stake in the event, helping to make sure the Fest is superbly
organized and enjoyable. Over 600 volunteers help man
the Fest to accommodate over 50,000 people who come to
Cape Cod from all over the country. Buses and trains bring
groups of people as well. It's the type of event that truly
brings everyone together for a great time." In fact, the Scallop
Festival has been cited by the American Bus Association as
one of "The Top 100 Events in North America" three times.

Because of the huge crowds, many people take the Cape

Cod Central Railroad, which offers "Ride the Rails" travel packages from Hyannis to Buzzards Bay.

Cape Cod is known for sea scallops and bay scallops. The scallops are used for the festival and available year-round. Cape or bay scallops are seasonal (October to April); They come from the deeper waters around the Cape. and are harvested in the bays and inlets.

For more information, visit bournescallopfest.com or call (508) 759-6000, ext.10.

ORIGINAL SCALLOP FEST DINNER RECIPE

Compliments of Joe Agrillo, Chief Cook

The Scallop Festival is an enormous event. To give you an idea of its scope, here is the recipe for the famous Scallop Dinner Recipe that feeds the crowds.

1,200 pounds flour

1,200 pounds clam fry mix

96 pounds nondairy creamer

18 gallons eggs, broken and ready

60 gallons water, warm

60 gallons water, cold

4,000 pounds vegetable shortening

6,000 pounds scallops

6,000 pounds french fries

3,500 pounds coleslaw

Special equipment: friolater

Thoroughly mix flour and clam fry mix in large shallow pan. Set aside.

Mix nondairy creamer and eggs with warm water and whip together until mixed thoroughly. Let stand 15 minutes at room temperature. Add cold water and whip thoroughly.

Heat shortening in friolater to 360°F frying temperature.

Place 2 cups scallops into a 10-inch-round wire mesh basket and dredge into flour and clam fry mix coating scallops well with the mixture. Shake well to remove excess flour.

Put coated scallops into egg wash mixture.
Place dipped scallops into first basket and dredge in flour and clam fry mix mixture a second time.
Place dredged scallops into fryer basket and cook in friolater until golden brown.
Place on paper towels to drain.
Continue this procedure repeatedly until all are cooked!
Serve with french fries and coleslaw.

The Glass Onion

The Glass Onion is located in the heart of Falmouth's Historic Queens Byway on Route 28 as you head into Falmouth Center. This elegant but casual restaurant is owned and operated by Josh and Tally Christian. I met Josh several years ago when he was a waiter at a restaurant in the mid-Cape area. At that time he had wishes and dreams about having his own place. Today his dreams have come true, and he has created one of the most consistent, high-end, stylish restaurants on the Cape, in the town where he was born.

Josh manages and runs the front of the house, while Tally is the behind-the-scenes manager, except on Friday and Saturday nights when she is in the front of the house with Josh. The three-year-old restaurant has received major raves for its inventive and delicious menu, professional service, comfortable atmosphere, and beautiful decor. Above the old, white Cape Cod wainscoting, the walls are painted lovely sea foam green. It is the perfect setting for a romantic dinner or special occasion. The Glass Onion is open for dinner only.

The Lobster Strudel, made with mascarpone, has become one of the restaurant's signature dishes. Another favorite is Oysters on the Half Shell, served with a cucumber mignonette sauce, lemon, and extra-virgin olive oil. The oysters are provided by a local oyster farmer, Les Hemmila of Barnstable Seafarms. Tally's mother, Sally Talmadge, is the bread maker for the restaurant, making thirty-five to forty loaves a day. And for dessert the Lavender Chèvre Cheesecake with Blueberry Compote should not be missed.

37 North Main Street, Falmouth, MA 02540, (508) 540-3730, theglassoniondining.com

LAVENDER CHÈVRE CHEESECAKE WITH BLUEBERRY COMPOTE

(Serves 12)

FOR THE CHEESECAKE:
12 ounces chèvre (goat cheese), room temperature
10 ounces cream cheese, room temperature
½ cup sugar
½ cup honey
¼ cup all-purpose flour
Zest and juice of 1 large orange (about 2 teaspoons zest and 3 tablespoons juice)
1 teaspoon finely chopped dried lavender buds
1 teaspoon kosher salt
8 eggs, separated, room temperature
1¼ cup mascarpone cheese
4 tablespoons sugar

To make the cheesecake: Preheat oven to 350°F. Generously butter 12 (8-ounce) ramekins and place side by side in a roasting pan just large enough to hold them all. Set aside. Bring a large pot of water to boil.

Combine the chèvre and cream cheese in the bowl of an electric mixer fitted with a paddle attachment. Beat on medium speed just until creamy and smooth, scraping down the sides of the bowl several times (do not overmix). Add the sugar, honey, flour, orange zest, lavender, and salt; mix just until thoroughly blended. With the mixer on low speed, add the egg yolks one at a time, beating just to incorporate before adding the next. Add the mascarpone and orange juice and continue beating just until thoroughly blended. Set batter aside.

Replace the mixer's paddle attachment with the whisk attachment and place the egg whites in a clean mixer bowl. Beat on medium speed until thick and foamy. Add the sugar, 1 tablespoon at a time, and continue beating until soft peaks form. Fold a third of the whites into the batter to lighten, then add the rest of the egg whites, folding quickly and carefully until no streaks remain.

Divide the batter among the prepared ramekins and place the roasting pan in the oven. Carefully add just enough boiling water to the roasting pan to come halfway up the outsides of the ramekins. Lay a sheet of aluminum foil lightly over the ramekins and bake until they just jiggle in the center, about 30 minutes. One at a time, carefully remove ramekins from the water bath and transfer to a wire rack to cool.

To make the compote: Put 1½ cups of blueberries, water, and sugar, in a medium saucepan, reserving ½ cup of the blueberries. Bring to a boil; reduce heat to medium and cook for 10 minutes.

Add remaining blueberries, lemon juice, and zest and cook for another 6 to 8 minutes.

Spoon the compote, 1 or 2 tablespoons, over each dessert before serving.

FOR THE COMPOTE
(YIELDS ABOUT 1 ½ CUPS):
2 cups fresh blueberries
3 tablespoons water
¼ cup granular sugar
2 tablespoons lemon juice
½ teaspoon lemon zest

LOBSTER STRUDEL

(Serves 8)

FOR THE LOBSTER FILLING:

8 ounces fresh lobster meat, diced

½ cup mascarpone cheese

Juice and zest of ½ large lemon

½ teaspoon chopped fresh tarragon

½ teaspoon chopped fresh parsley

½ teaspoon chopped fresh chives

Salt and pepper to taste

FOR THE STRUDEL:

1 (16-ounce) box phyllo dough, thawed

½ cup unsalted butter, melted

FOR THE SAUCE:

½ cup lobster stock (page 136)

2 tablespoons heavy cream

½ cup unsalted butter, cut in cubes and softened

Fresh lemon juice to taste

Salt and pepper to taste

For the lobster filling: Combine the lobster, cheese, lemon juice and zest, and herbs in a bowl. Toss gently until evenly mixed; season with salt and pepper to taste. Cover and refrigerate until needed.

For the strudel: Preheat oven to 475°F. Stack 2 sheets of phyllo on a large clean, dry work surface. With a pastry brush, very lightly coat the entire surface of the dough with melted butter.

Using a sharp knife, cut the dough in half crosswise to make two 9 x 14 rectangles. Place ⅛ of the lobster filling along the bottom (short side) of each rectangle, leaving about a ½-inch border all around. Fold the bottom border of dough up and over the length of the lobster filling, then fold in the sides. Carefully and evenly roll up the dough jelly roll style to completely enclose the filling. Repeat the process three more times to make 8 strudels in all.

Arrange strudels seam side down on a parchment-lined baking sheet so they are not touching and brush with melted butter. Bake until golden brown, about 6 to 8 minutes.

For the sauce: Combine stock and cream in saucepan over medium heat and bring to a simmer. Cook until thickened and reduced to about 3 tablespoons. Remove from heat and whisk in butter, a little at a time, until incorporated. Season to taste with lemon juice and salt and pepper.

To assemble the dish: Place one strudel on each serving plate and spoon sauce over it. Serve immediately.

All About Oysters
How Do You Like Your Oysters?

There are as many toppings for oysters on the half shell as there are oysters. I asked a couple of chefs for their favorites.

From Florence Lowell, *Chef/Owner at Naked Oyster (page 124)*

CUCUMBER SAKE AND GINGER MIGNONETTE

½ cucumber with skin, finely diced

1 teaspoon freshly grated ginger root

Salt and black pepper to taste

1 cup premium sake

Add ingredients to sake. Chill for 2 hours before topping chilled oysters with a teaspoon of sauce.

From Michael Ceraldi, *Chef/Owner at Ceraldi's (page 151)*

PROSECCO GRANITA

1 bottle Prosecco

2 whole shallots, peeled

2 fresh bay leaves

¼ cup granulated sugar

½ teaspoon salt

Pomegranate seeds

Combine all ingredients in a saucepan over medium-low heat and reduce by half. Remove the bay leaves and shallots. Pour liquid into shallow plastic storage container and place in the freezer for 4 to 6 hours, until frozen solid. Using a metal spoon, scrape the top of the frozen ice, pulling the spoon toward you, to create the granita. The scraped granita can be stored in the freezer in another plastic storage container, or it can be scraped as needed.

Top each chilled oyster with the granita and several pomegranate seeds and serve.

Shucking Oysters

You will need a real oyster knife found in any hardware or fish market on the Cape. Gloves are advised, at least one on the hand that is holding the oyster, but a towel will work just as well. I have found it's best to put the oysters in the freezer for about 15 minutes before shucking.

If using a small towel, drape it in your hand over the oyster, flat side up, or place it on a firm surface. Make sure to hold the oyster firmly. Slip the point of the knife between the top and bottom shells between the hinge.

Using a twisting motion, pry the two shells apart, making sure not to lose any of the liquid inside.

Run the knife around the top shell until you get to the other side. This will sever the tendon on the top of the shell.

Slide the knife under the oyster to cut it free from its shell (it will be connected by a tough knob). Place the oyster on a bed of crushed ice and serve with your favorite topping.

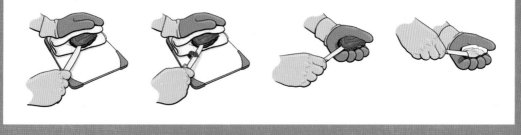

Illustrations by Robert Prince

Wellfleet OysterFest

The Wellfleet OysterFest is a two-day (Saturday and Sunday) event held the weekend after Columbus Day in a variety of locations across Wellfleet. It is produced by Shellfish Promotion and Tasting (SPAT), a nonprofit organization devoted to fostering a greater understanding of the history and traditions of the town's shellfishing industry. The acronym honors the oyster, which begins life as a free-swimming larva called spat. SPAT is also committed to educating the public about preserving traditional shellfishing practices and the creation of new shellfishing technologies.

The OysterFest began in 2001 and now includes seminars, a shucking contest, a 5K road race, an arts and crafts fair, and cooking demonstrations. You can also choose to spend the entire weekend in and around Town Hall, sampling the wide variety of foods supplied by Cape restaurants and food vendors. Hot foods, cold foods, and raw foods are all there. There's also fine dining, informal dining, and music. The schedule of events is posted at the website, and a visit there is essential.

Mac Hay is the owner of Mac's Shack in Wellfleet and president of SPAT's board of directors. He says, "The OysterFest provides and enhances a way of bringing the Wellfleet community together as well as preserving an important way of life here. It also brings people in. This is great exposure for the Lower Cape on what otherwise would be a down, off-season weekend. Most activities and restaurants end and close after Columbus Day. This event extends the season a little. It's the big fall finale before we go into the winter months here on the Cape."

For more information visit wellfleetoysterfest.org.

Green Briar Jam Kitchen

The Jam Kitchen dates back to 1903, when Ida Putman, the original owner, inherited her mother's house in East Sandwich. Ida decided to open a tearoom and served tea, toast, sandwiches, and cake. It was not a success. Ida didn't have much experience in the kitchen and in truth was not a good cook. However, her preserves were a hit, so Ida got herself a copy of *Fannie Farmer* and taught herself the art of preserving fruit.

Ida's perseverance for making jams and jellies paid off. The business continued to grow. Martha Blake started working in the kitchen when she was seventeen and purchased the business from Ida Putman thirty years later. In 1977 Martha celebrated her seventy-fifth birthday and wanted to retire. She was single-handedly putting up eleven thousand jars of preserves a season and ready to sell. But unfortunately there were no takers. In 1979 the Thornton W. Burgess Society, a fledging environmental education organization based in Sandwich, bought it. The society didn't plan to keep it as a jam kitchen, but Martha donated Ida's original recipes in the event that someday they might be put to use. Then in 1980 the Society decided to reopen the Jam Kitchen, and the building was back in full operation. Martha came back and volunteered her services until she was into her nineties. She died on July 6, 2002.

Mizue Murphy worked under Martha Blake in the kitchen and is still there today guarding most of the recipe secrets.

Visiting the Green Briar Jam Kitchen is a major treat in many ways. Take a tour and you'll be able to experience the fragrant aromas of fruits and preserves coming from the kettles used by Ida and Martha as they simmer on the old black burners. Observe the sun-cooked fruits under the glass structure in the gift shop. This is a place where time stands still and a tradition is kept alive.

Thornton W. Burgess Society, 6 Discovery Hill Road, East Sandwich, MA 02567, (508) 888-6870, thorntonburgess.org

SUN-COOKED PEACHES

(Makes 6 pints)

4 pounds peaches
4 pounds sugar (about 9 cups)
1 cup brandy

To skin the peaches, cut an X through just the skin on the bottom of each one. Put peaches in boiling water until skins loosen a bit, 20 to 60 seconds. (Riper peaches require less time.) Transfer peaches to a bowl of ice water. One at a time, lift peaches out of the water bath and slip off the skins. Remove pits and slice fruit to ½-inch thickness.

Combine peaches and sugar in a shallow enamel or a glass pan. Cover with a clear glass lid or plastic wrap and place in full sun for several days in a protected area. At the end of the cooking process, pour brandy over the fruit. Pour into 8-ounce sterilized jars and process to seal.

BREAD & BUTTER PICKLES

(Makes about 2 pints)

2 English or 5 pickling-size
   cucumbers
6 small white (boiling) onions
   peeled and thinly sliced
2 tablespoons coarse pickling
   salt
3 cups white grape juice
   simmered and reduced by half
⅔ cup cider vinegar
⅓ teaspoon whole mustard seed
¼ teaspoon celery seed
½ teaspoon black pepper
¼ teaspoon turmeric powder
1 cup sugar

Scour the cucumbers lengthwise with the tines of fork. Slice crosswise ⅜-inch thick.

Put cucumbers, onions, and pickling salt in a bowl and toss to coat. Let stand for 30 minutes then rinse in cold water. Transfer to a large non-aluminum pot then add the grape juice, vinegar, spices, and sugar. Bring to a boil over high heat, stirring to dissolve the sugar. Boil 5 minutes and remove from heat. Pour into two sterilized pint jars and seal.

Italian Gourmet Foods/ "Slice Of Italy"

You do not have to go to Boston's North End to find quality Italian foods and products—it is all here in Falmouth. Nedo's Slice of Italy is filled with all the things you find in Boston's Little Italy. His two kinds of Italian homemade sausages, hot and mild, are the best!

One whole isle is dedicated to several brands of dried pastas. In back, Nedo Jr. serves slices and whole pizzas, calzones, and domestic and imported cold cuts. He also prepares hot meals to go; there is a freezer on one wall full of frozen prepared meals like stuffed shells, lasagna with tomato sauce, and manicotti—all enough for small or large parties.

As I moved around the store next to the frozen prepared foods, I found the imported and domestic cheeses and special dried sausages. There I found 'nduja, the spicy pork spread famous in southern Italy which can be used as an appetizer. Alternatively, you can stir a few tablespoons in a red sauce and toss with penne pasta for a delicious meal. Nedo is quite proud of his own brand of imported olive oil with "Slice of Italy" on the label.

I could not leave the store without having a cannoli filled with Nedo's fresh ricotta cream filling. Slice of Italy is a place to explore; you would feel you were in the North End in Boston!

890 Main Street, Falmouth, MA 02540, (508) 495-1106

CREAMY CHICKEN MARSALA

Flour for dredging
salt and pepper to taste
4 boneless chicken breasts
2 tablespoon butter
1 tablespoon olive oil
8 oz baby bella mushrooms
2 cloves of garlic minced
¾ cup Marsala wine
¾ cup low salt chicken broth
⅓ heavy cream
2 tbsp freshly chopped parsley
   or basil

For the chicken: Season flour with salt and pepper and dredge chicken in flour. In large skillet over medium heat, melt 1 tablespoon of butter and 1 tablespoon olive oil. Cook chicken until golden brown.

For the Marsala sauce: Melt remaining butter in skillet and add mushrooms. Cook until mushrooms are golden and liquid has been released, 7–9 min. Add garlic and stir until fragrant; sprinkle with salt to taste.

Add Marsala, chicken broth, heavy cream, and parsley to mushrooms and bring to a simmer.

Return chicken to skillet and spoon sauce over breast.

Simmer until chicken is cooked through, about 12 minutes.

Serve alone or over pasta

The Lobster Trap

The Lobster Trap was founded in 1969 as a neighborhood fish market on Old County Road in Bourne. Dave Delaney started working as a chef in 1998 for the previous owner when the owner decided to expand and open a restaurant. Dave bought the establishment in 2003, enlarged the restaurant, started a catering business, and formed a distribution company which serves restaurants and markets worldwide.

In 2008 Dave brought in his brother Daniel as executive chef. Daniel and his team create simple, approachable dishes, bursting with natural flavors. Offerings include classics like lobster rolls and fish & chips, as well as a change of pace like an upscale crab cakes and tuna pad Thai "There's something on our menu for everyone!" exclaims Daniel.

"We are committed to providing guests with the best possible products we can source, prepared with care and served with pride. After all, this isn't just a job for us, it's a way of life," adds Dave.

The Lobster Trap is a true Cape Cod experience. One can take in the view of Buzzards Bay, the Back River, and surrounding saltwater marshes, while having a cold brew or margarita at the bar or lunch or dinner in the large dining room. The patio is open during the spring and summer months, a perfect place to relax with friends and family.

290 Shore Road, Bourne, MA 02532, (508) 759-7600, lobstertrap.net

FISH & CHIPS

(Serves 1)

Here is a rough approximation of the recipe Chef Dan Delaney uses in the restaurant. The recipe may be doubled.

½ pound dayboat cod
1 egg beaten with 3 tablespoons
  cold water (egg wash)
Your favorite Clam fry mix
Vegetable oil for frying

Place fish in egg wash and then the clam fry mix. Repeat a second time. Using a large pan, add the oil, enough to cover the fish, heat to 375°F. Add fish and fry for 3 to 4 minutes. Drain on paper towel. Salt and pepper to taste. Serve with French fries, your favorite coleslaw, and a lemon wedge.

LOBSTER TRAP CRAB CAKE

(Serves 4)

1 pound jumbo lump crab meat
½ red pepper, diced small
½ green pepper, diced small
¼ red onion, diced small
5 ounces crushed Ritz crackers
3 ounces panko bread crumbs
½ bunch cilantro, chopped fine
½ bunch scallions, chopped fine
2 tablespoons Dijon-style
   mustard
½ cup mayonnaise
Salt and pepper to taste

FOR AVOCADO CREAM:
2 ripe avocados, peeled and
   pitted
¼ cup sour cream
Juice of 1 lime
Salt and pepper to taste

FOR MANGO SALSA:
½ ripe mango, skin removed,
   diced small
½ red pepper, diced small
½ green pepper, diced small
¼ red onion, diced small
½ bunch cilantro
½ bunch scallions
Juice of 1 lime

Fold all ingredients together and make cakes. Place on a lightly greased cookie sheet and bake in a preheated 350°F oven for 10 minutes.

Place each crab cake on a plate, drizzle with avocado cream, and top with the mango salsa.

AVOCADO CREAM

Place ingredients into food processor or blender and blend until smooth.

MANGO SALSA

Mix all ingredients together in a medium bowl.

Maison Villatte

On November 2012, the French bakery-café Maison Villatte opened in Falmouth. Spanish tiles line the floor, and there are wooden beams on the ceiling of this spacious, warm, and friendly café and bakery. To the right, displayed in a glass case one cannot avoid, are incredibly gorgeous pastries. Behind a wall filled with Villatte's famous breads, I found Boris, who developed his knowledge and artistry under Eric Kayser, the internationally known French baker. Boris traveled for six years for Kayser, opening boulangeries around the globe.

While I was there, it was lunch time. I decided to have a sandwich and looked at the end of the counter to see what was offered that day. The one that caught my eye was the La Romana. I later found out it was the invention of Valentin Pellat, Boris's bread-making assistant, also from France. I had the opportunity to talk to Valentin about the sandwich I selected and wondered how it got its name.

Valentin explained, "I spent time working in Emilia-Romagna, in Italy, and I named the sandwich La Romana for the place and the cheese, Pecorino Romano."

Here is the recipe Valentin gave me:

"I use the fresh focaccia bread we bake ever morning. It is cut to the sandwich size (about 4 x 4 inches). I spread the sundried tomato and basil pesto on each slice of the bread. For the pesto, I start with a basic basil pesto: basil, with fresh garlic, pine nuts, and olive oil then add sundried tomatoes and more olive oil if necessary. All this is done in a blender. Then a layer of prosciutto goes next, fresh arugula, and sliced Pecorino cheese."

267 Main Street, Falmouth, MA 02540, (744) 255-1855

Nonna Elena
"Un Negozio Italiano"

Here is a place for quality imported Italian goods with no artificial ingredients. Most are from small farmers and producers. Nonna Elena carries antipasti, artichokes, Italian tuna, a variety of cheeses, sauces (puttanesca, pesto, and artichoke), and good breads.

On your way home and want to create a simple meal? Pick up an antipasto, one of their pastas (and there are many!), a jar of sauce, and a loaf of bread––and there is dinner!

598 Route 6A, East Sandwich, MA 02537, (508) 744-7062, Nonnaelenaimports.com

Nobska Farms

I first met Rooster Fricke a few years ago at the local farmers' market in Falmouth. At that time, one of the restaurants he was supplying with his peppers was Quicks Hole Taquiera in Woods Hole.

I made a special trip to visit Rooster and his wife Susanne for a private tour of their wonderful gardens of peppers. "We specialize in exotic, rare, hard-to-find chili peppers and related products for commercial sale." As we were walking around the property, Rooster continued, "All of the peppers are grown using organic methods, and we are always on the lookout for new and interesting varieties. This year we grew about 80 varieties of chili peppers. Over the past several years, we've grown about 300 varieties. We are always experimenting with new types and selecting the ones we like to keep growing in the future."

Along with the chillies, he produces everything from hot and spicy salsas and sauces to two kinds of chocolate products, as well as jellies. Chili enthusiasts and regional chefs are all buying their chillies and rely on Nobska Farms to satisfy their need for heat, spice, and flavor.

For fans of chocolate and spice, check out the Mexican Oatmeal Chocolate Chip Cookies on the following page.

9 Nobska Road, Woods Hole, MA 02543, (617) 480-0876, nobskafarms.com

MEXICAN OATMEAL CHOCOLATE CHIP COOKIES

(Yield 5 Dozen 1 ½ Inch Cookies)

"Folks ask how we use our Demon Dust chillies. We have lots of ways, but here's a recipe from one of our customers. It blends spicy with sweet. Awesome flavor with just the right touch of heat. Here goes!"

1¼ cups old-fashioned rolled oats
¾ cup all-purpose flour
½ teaspoon baking soda
½ teaspoon ground cinnamon (or maybe a bit more)
¼ teaspoon salt
¼ teaspoon Demon Dust chillies (less for less bite ... more for, well, more bite!)
Sunflower seeds (optional)
½ cup unsalted butter (1 stick)
⅔ cup brown sugar (dark or dark/ light mix)
2 teaspoons vanilla extract
1 large egg, beaten
3-4 ounces dark chocolate, crushed into chip-sized chunks

Preheat oven to 325°F. Whisk oats, flour, baking soda, cinnamon, salt, Demon Dust, and sunflower seeds together in a bowl. Beat butter until creamy in an electric mixer on medium-high speed; add brown sugar gradually. Continue beating until light and fluffy. Beat in vanilla until well mixed, and then beat in the egg. Add about ⅓ of the oat and flour mix at low speed. Gradually add remaining flour until well blended, and finally the chocolate chunks. Bake cookies on parchment paper for about 13 minutes. Place cookies and parchment paper on rack to cool.

Gather friends and family, share, and enjoy. Goes beautifully with a nice cup of coffee (lots of cream) or vanilla ice cream sandwiches!

Note: For thinner, wider cookies, bake immediately; for thicker cookies, chill dough for at least 2 hours.

Osterville Fish

I live a few miles from Osterville Fish. It is the closest place to my home to buy local fresh fish. If I go there around lunch or dinner time, I notice people waiting to pick up their daily specials, cooked in the kitchen by Sam Monroe or another staff member. Paul Dean, the owner, has created a friendly environment, as you can readily experience when you walk into the market.

2952 Falmouth Road (Route 28), Osterville, MA 02655, (508) 420-0500, Ostervillefish.com

AHI TUNA TACO

(Makes 1 Taco)

FOR THE SLAW:

1 small red onion, diced
¼ of a head of red cabbage,
    sliced thin
1 small sweet red pepper, cut
    into strips
2 carrots shredded
1 small cucumber, diced
Wasabi dressing (Can be
    purchased at Osterville Fish)

FOR THE TUNA:

5 ounces sushi-grade tuna
Toasted sesame seeds
Corn or flour tortilla, charred
    slightly over an open flame
Oil for cooking

To make the slaw: In a medium bowl, combine the red onion, red cabbage, sweet red pepper, carrots, and cucumber, and stir in the wasabi dressing. Set aside.

To make the tuna taco: Brush a little oil on the tuna, then roll it in the sesame seeds, making sure tuna is totally coated. In a medium frying pan, pour enough oil to cover the bottom of the pan. Heat the oil and once hot, place the tuna in the pan, and sear for about 1-3 minutes per side to desired doneness. Place the cooked tuna on the taco and top with a handful of slaw. Fold the taco in half and serve.

LOCAL !!
FRESH !!

★ MORNING GLORY FARM -MARTHA'S VINEYARD

★ ATLANTIC OYSTER -WAQUOIT

★ CLAM MAN -FALMOUTH

★ ALLEN FARMS -WESTPORT

★ COONAMESSET FARMS -FALMOUTH

★ NOBSKA FARM -WOODS HOLE

★ NOT YOUR SUGAR MAMAS -MARTHA'S VINEYARD

Quicks Hole Taqueria

This seasonal farm-to-table restaurant is on the ground floor of the Woods Hole Inn and sits on a corner facing the Woods Hole Ferry. The building, built in 1898, was for sale and in dire need of repair. Beth Colt, formerly in the entertainment business in Los Angeles, bought the building and opened the restaurant and inn. Here you'll find the commitment to using local ingredients illustrated in their salads and seafood, especially the Sippewissett, Cuttyhunk, and Washburn Island oysters.

Former Chef Stephanie Mastroianni comes from a family of commercial fishermen in a small port town in Rhode Island. Several years spent living on the West Coast gave her a very Californian take on New England traditions and created quite a buzz around this unique restaurant. "The menu is 100 percent mine. My lobster tacos are one of the specialties of the house, but I make other seafood, pork and chicken burritos, quesadillas, and salads says Mastroianni." For drinks, try the special cold sangria or a chilled local beer.

If you are there in the early evening you can eat, drink, and watch the spectacular sunset over the harbor. And if you are a cycling enthusiast, take the eight-mile Shining Sea Bikeway from Bourne to Woods Hole. You'll pass sandy beaches, salt marshes, and shoreside ponds before emerging at Little Harbor in Woods Hole. Have lunch at Quicks Hole and then hop back on the trail.

6 Luscombe Avenue, Woods Hole, MA 02543, (508) 495-0792, quicksholewickedfresh.com

LOBSTER TACOS

(Serves 6)

FOR THE LOBSTER:

3 pounds fresh lobster meat,
  cut into bite-size pieces
1 cup mayonnaise
½ cup chopped fresh basil or
  tarragon
¼ cup fresh lemon or lime juice
  (from 1 lemon or 2 limes)
Salt and pepper to taste

FOR THE PICO DE GALLO:

6 Roma tomatoes, seeded and
  diced
1 cup diced red onion
1 cup chopped fresh cilantro
½ cup fresh lime juice
  (from 2 limes)
3 garlic cloves, finely chopped
Salt and pepper to taste

FOR THE BAJA SAUCE:

1 cup sour cream
1 cup chopped fresh cilantro
½ cup mayonnaise
½ cup fresh lime juice
  (from 2 limes)
3 poblano peppers, charred,
  peeled, stemmed, seeded,
  and chopped
2 tablespoons hot sauce

12 (6-inch) corn or flour tortillas
½ small head green cabbage,
  cored and shredded
Queso fresco (Mexican farmer's
  cheese), or regular farmer's
  cheese

For the lobster: Combine the lobster meat, mayonnaise, basil, and lemon or lime juice in a bowl and toss gently until evenly mixed. Add salt and pepper to taste. Set aside.

For the pico de gallo: Combine the ingredients in a bowl and mix well. Season with salt and pepper and set aside.

For the Baja sauce: Place the ingredients in a food processor fitted with a steel blade and blend until smooth. Transfer mixture to a squeeze bottle.

To assemble the dish: Place 2 tortillas on each plate. Mound some cabbage on each tortilla. Divide the lobster meat among the tortillas and top each with 2 to 3 tablespoons pico de gallo, a sprinkle of *queso fresco,* and a drizzle of Baja sauce.

Most of the food at Quicks Hole is served with their famous Sangria.

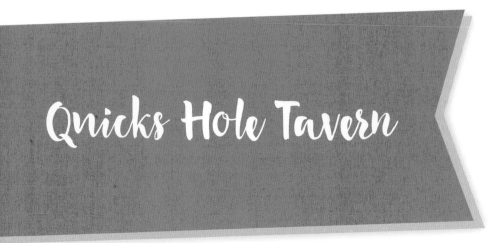

Quicks Hole Tavern

The Quicks Hole Tavern, like its sister Quicks Hole Taqueria next door, is committed to farm-to-table sourcing and boasts "wicked fresh" local ingredients. The menu changes with the seasons and offers original twists on local seafood, cheese and charcuterie boards, burgers, gourmet grilled-cheese sandwiches, and freshly made soups and salads––plus an extensive craft beer list, a fine selection of wines, and a full bar.

29 Railroad Avenue, Woods Hole, MA 02543, (508) 495-0048, Open year round

CORN NUT ENCRUSTED SEA SCALLOPS
SUMMER SUCCOTASH AND HERBED BACON SALAD
(Serves 6)

FOR THE SUMMER SUCCOTASH:
¼ cup butter
1 large onion, diced medium
6 cloves garlic, minced
10 ears of corn, shucked and
    kernels removed
2 zucchini, medium diced
2 summer squash, medium diced
2 sweet red peppers, medium
    diced
1 cup shelled edamame
1 teaspoon thyme leaves
1 teaspoon rosemary leaves
White wine for deglazing
¾ cup heavy cream

FOR THE HERBED BACON
    SALAD:
½ pound slab bacon or thick cut
    bacon, cut into ¼-inch pieces
1 bunch chives, roughly chopped
1 bunch whole cilantro leaves,
    stems removed
1 bunch whole flat leaf parsley
    leaves, stems removed
3 tablespoons olive oil

FOR THE SCALLOPS:
2 pounds sea scallops
1 cup of roasted corn nuts
(blended fine in food processor)

To make the succotash: Sauté onions in butter until translucent. Add garlic and cook for 2 minutes. Add corn, zucchini, squash, pepper and edamame. Cook until al dente. Add herbs then white wine. Add heavy cream and bring to a slow boil. Season with salt and pepper. Simmer 5-10 minutes in cream until thickened slightly.

To make the herbed bacon salad: In another pan sauté the bacon pieces on medium heat cooking all the fat out and crisping the bacon. Set aside. To make the salad, toss the crispy bacon bits and herbs together with olive oil, salt, and pepper.

To prepare the scallops: Encrust the scallops with the corn nuts and salt and pepper, and place in a hot sauté pan with oil. Sear on one side for 3 minutes. After 1½ minutes, add 1 tablespoon of butter to caramelize the scallops. Turn the scallops over, and cook for another minute or so.

To finish the dish: Pour the succotash on the bottom of the plate. Place the herb and bacon salad in the center, and position the scallops around the salad.

Sagamore Inn

The Sagamore Inn dates back to the 1930s. While it has not functioned as an inn since the early part of the last century, it still retains the charm of its past. The dining room, which seats about 125, has its original tin ceiling, and some of the walls are tongue-in-groove paneling. A NO DANCING sign from World War II is still tacked on the wall next to the bar. The beautiful wood floors are sanded and polished each spring. For many years the inn was run as a pizza business by owners Fiorello (Bill) and Severona Bianco, who were from the Piedmont region of Italy. Eventually they wanted to retire, but they also wanted to keep the business going, so the inn was rented to Shirley and Joseph (Paddy) Pagliarani, both natives of Cape Cod. In an interview Shirley, now eighty-five, sat in my kitchen and told me stories about the early days at the inn.

"At that time Paddy did not have ten cents in his pocket, so we kept the pizza business going. I started to work on other main dishes for the restaurant menu, mostly Italian dishes and seafood. I even dug quahogs (clams) for my chowder. I was at the restaurant at five thirty every morning making all the sauces, soups, chowders, and my signature dish—forty-five pounds of pot roast with my 'bodacious' gravy. Paddy managed and cooked in the kitchen. This was not just a two-person operation—it was a family affair; we had forty-three local people working for us, and many of our children would also pitch in."

Shirley and Paddy ran the inn for forty-five years. It was sold to Suzanne and Michael Biladeau just before Paddy passed away. The new owners preserved the original feel of the inn, with seafood platters, Italian pasta dishes, eggplant Parmesan, and Shirley's Yankee Pot Roast, which still appears on the menu along with the traditional bread and grape nut custard puddings.

1131 Route 6A, Sagamore, MA 02561, (508) 888-9707, sagamoreinncapecod.com

SAGAMORE INN'S GRAPE NUT CUSTARD PUDDING

(Serves 8–10)

1 cup Post Grape Nuts Cereal
4 cups warm milk
4 large eggs, beaten
¾ cup granulated sugar
¼ teaspoon salt
1 teaspoon pure vanilla extract
½ teaspoon ground cinnamon or
 ¼ teaspoon nutmeg (or both)

Preheat oven to 350°F.

Put the cereal in a medium-size bowl and pour the milk over it. Let stand 5 minutes.

In another medium-size bowl, add the eggs, sugar, salt, vanilla, and cinnamon and/or nutmeg. Whisk until well combined.

Add the milk and cereal to the egg mixture and stir well. Pour into a buttered 9 x 13 x 2-inch baking dish set inside a larger pan filled with hot water (called a bain-marie or water bath). Bake about 45 to 60 minutes or until a knife inserted in center comes out clean.

SHIRLEY'S YANKEE POT ROAST

(Serves 6)

FOR THE ROAST:

4–5 pound beef boneless chuck
   roast (For best results,
   look for a piece that is well
   marbled with fat.)
Salt and pepper to taste
2 tablespoons olive oil or
   rendered beef fat
1½ cups coarsely chopped
   onions
1½ cups coarsely chopped
   carrots
1½ cups coarsely chopped
   celery
½ cup water

FOR THE GRAVY:

¾ cup cold water
3 tablespoons all-purpose flour

For the roast: Season the roast generously with salt and pepper. Heat the oil in an 8-quart deep-sided cast iron pot or Dutch oven over high heat and carefully add the meat to the pan. Sear well on all sides; transfer to a plate.

Add onions to the pan drippings and cook, stirring, until golden and translucent, about 5 minutes. Return meat to the pan along with the carrots, celery, water, and salt and pepper to taste. Bring to a boil, cover the pot, and adjust the heat to a simmer. Cook, turning occasionally, until meat is tender, about 4 hours. Remove from heat. Remove the meat and vegetables from the braising liquid and discard the vegetables.

For the gravy: Return the pot to high heat and bring the braising liquid to a boil. Place the water in a small bowl and gradually add the flour, whisking constantly to form a smooth slurry. Add the slurry to the boiling liquid gradually, whisking constantly until mixture thickens to gravy consistency.

Return the meat to the pan to heat through. Slice the roast and serve with the gravy over mashed potatoes. This is what Shirley calls her "Bodacious Gravy."

The Seafood Shanty

A good place to begin your Cape Cod adventure is The Seafood Shanty in Bournedale, along the Cape Cod Canal. Located almost at the midpoint between the Sagamore and Bourne Bridges, the Seafood Shanty is one of the Cape's best-kept secrets. You'll find a delicious lobster roll filled with tender chunks of lobster and just enough mayonnaise. It's what a lobster roll should be, simple and traditional. It is served on a toasted hot dog roll with a side of coleslaw or french fries.

Tish (short for Patricia) and Johnny Economides have run this seasonal business for over twenty-two years. Family-run until the kids struck out on their own, today Tish and Johnny operate the Shanty with a group of students. Johnny has worked in restaurants all his life and does the cooking. "My parents owned a business in Falmouth called Joan and Ted's in the 1960s." Take a look in the back of the Shanty and you can see the sign. "I make and serve the food the way we like it. That goes for the portion size and the way it is presented. Everything is homemade and made to order. All our fish and shellfish are fresh and bought from local vendors."

Order your food, sit in one of the Adirondack chairs, and take in the view of the boats passing by on the Canal. The portions are generous, and the service is fast and efficient. They don't serve alcohol, but you're welcome to bring your own beer or wine. You won't find a more perfect setting!

803 Scenic Highway, Route 6, Bournedale, MA 02532, (508) 888-0040, theseafoodshanty.net

LOBSTER ROLL
(Serves 1)

8 ounces freshly cooked lobster
  meat, cut in bite-size pieces
½–1 teaspoon mayonnaise
Salt and pepper to taste
1 large leaf romaine or Boston
  lettuce
1 hot dog roll, buttered and
  toasted golden

Place the lobster meat in a bowl and add the mayonnaise, salt and pepper, tossing to coat. Tuck the lettuce leaf lengthwise into the bottom of the roll, pile the lobster meat over the lettuce, and serve with a cold beer from Cape Cod Beer Company (page 86).

Water Street Kitchen

The new kids on the block are the Wilsons, who took over what use to be The Fishmonger in Woods Hole. The restaurant sits next to the drawbridge and looks onto the water leading into the harbor. The place has been renovated but still has the same charming and rustic Cape Cod atmosphere, now with a more "together" feel. Wilson worked as chef at The Glass Onion and the Quicks Hole Tavern before he and Molly decided to open their own place. Woods Hole has become a foodie destination.

The night we were there, we sat by the window where we could see boats below going in and out of the harbor. There is a cozy bar managed by Molly's sister Chelsea. It's a great place to have a drink and eat on a cold winter night. The menu changes with the seasons, and Wilson puts his own twist on familiar dishes with a slight Asian or Indian flavor. His food is delicious!

56 Water Street, Woods Hole, MA 20543, (508) 540-5656, waterstreetkitchen.com

TUNA TARTARE
(Serves 4)

This dish is all about beautiful, fresh ingredients. Buy the freshest tuna you can find. (A good fishmonger, if asked, will help you find the best fish for consuming raw.) The fresh herbs also elevate this tartare. You can eat it with crostini if you like, but the clean crunch of a cucumber slice is all you need to let all the elements shine through in perfect harmony. Use a 3-inch ring mold, if available, for shaping the presentation.

1 pound cleaned and trimmed
    sushi grade tuna
1 tablespoon finely chopped
    basil
2 teaspoons finely chopped mint
½ small jalapeno pepper, finely
    chopped
Zest of 1 lemon
2 teaspoons olive oil
2 teaspoon lemon oil
Sea salt to taste
10 slices English cucumber
Pea greens and/or arugula
Lemon juice
Extra olive oil

Place tuna in freezer for 30-45 minutes (so it will dice cleanly). Remove tuna from freezer and dice into 1/8-inch cubes. Place diced tuna in a bowl and mix in herbs, jalapeño, lemon zest, olive and lemon oils, and salt. Divide the tuna mixture among 4 plates, optionally using a ring mold to form it, or portion into small bowls. Sprinkle a generous pinch of salt over tuna mixture on each plate. In a medium mixing bowl, mix 1 part lemon juice to 2 parts olive oil and toss with the greens. Finish plates with dressed greens and cucumber slices.

MID CAPE

Brazilian Grill

It's called the Brazilian Grill and serves Churrascaria, which means "Rotisserie Barbeque." This wonderfully unique restaurant is located in the west end of Hyannis, and you will not find a dining experience like it anywhere else on Cape Cod.

The creative force behind this twelve-year-old restaurant is Massimiliano De Paulo. "I have been in this country for twenty years and started working in restaurants washing dishes, then as a chef," he says. "I have been saving my money since I arrived here. A large Brazilian community exists on Cape Cod, and I found the opportunity to open this restaurant."

When you enter the restaurant, you immediately feel the warmth and helpfulness of the staff. Ranato, the headwaiter, suggests a caipirinha, the national cocktail of Brazil, to start. He then explains the ordering system: On each table are small round tokens. "It works like a traffic light. On one side are red and the other green. When you are ready for your meat course, turn your token to the green side and one of the servers, or gauchos, will come to your table with a knife and skewer, on which are speared various kinds of meat. We have ten to fifteen cuts of meat; beef, pork, chicken, and lamb are the most popular. The meat is cut, the pieces roll off the knife, and you pick up the small tongs next to your plate and bring the meat to your plate. When finished, turn the token to the red side." This is important to remember, because the Brazilian Grill offers a fixed-price, all-you-can-eat menu. At the rear of the restaurant you'll find a buffet with a variety of salads, vegetables, grains, sliced meats, soups, and even sushi. The butternut squash soup is a favorite of Chef De Paulo's. There's also a number of traditional Brazilian favorites, such as rice and beans, sausages, and fried bananas. And, of course, a large selection of desserts. Everything is made fresh and in-house. Bring your appetite and enjoy a bit of Brazil on Cape Cod.

680 Main Street, Hyannis, MA 02601, (508) 771-0109, braziliangrill-capecod.com

CAIPIRINHA

(Serves 1)

1 or 2 limes, quartered
2 teaspoons superfine sugar
2 ounces cachaca

Place the lime wedges and sugar into an Old Fashioned glass and crush the lime into the sugar. Fill the glass with ice cubes. Pour in the cachaca and stir well.

Cape Cod Beer Company, Inc.

In 1998 Beth and Todd Marcus moved from Philadelphia to Cape Cod to be closer to their families. Todd has a degree in electrical engineering, but his real passion has been in the breweries; at one time it was his hobby. His new career started when he answered an ad for a brewmaster at Hyannisport Brewing Company (HBC) in Hyannis. At the time it was the only local brewery in the area. It was a microbrewery with a restaurant attached to it. Todd got the job and worked there for five years, until the brewer closed its doors.

Beth and Todd decided to buy the equipment and start their own business here on the Cape. They are now in their ninth year.

"We are all about local and think of ourselves as champions of all things local!" Beth explains. They keep the distribution within a fifty-mile radius of the brewery to make sure the product is kept fresh. "We are passionate about our product, to say the least. It's like our first child," she goes on to say.

For Beth and Todd it is all about customer service, quality, community, and conservation. But some say, "It's all about the marketing," and while they don't disagree, it's really about their passion for their beer!

The Marcuses open the brewery to the public for guided tours. Check their website for hours of operation. And while you are there, take home a gallon of their delicious beer.

1336 Phinney's Lane, Hyannis, MA 02601, (508) 790-4200, capecodbeer.com

SPENT GRAIN CHEESE CRACKERS

(Makes about 8 dozen crackers)

2 cups (16 ounces) grated sharp
    cheddar cheese
½ cup (1 stick) unsalted butter,
    cut in pieces
1 cup all-purpose flour
¼ teaspoon salt
Cayenne pepper to taste
½ cup chopped pecans
½ cup spent grain

Combine the cheese and butter in a food processor fitted with a steel blade. Process until well blended. Add the flour, salt, and cayenne; pulse to blend. Add the pecans and spent grain and pulse several times to evenly incorporate. Do not overprocess the dough; it should be crumbly, not creamy, with visible bits of pecans.

Turn the dough out onto a sheet of parchment or waxed paper on a work surface. Shape the dough into a log about 1½ inches in diameter, wrap in plastic, and refrigerate for at least 1 hour.

Preheat oven to 350°F. Unwrap the chilled dough and place on a cutting board. With a sharp knife, slice the dough into ⅛-inch-thick rounds and arrange ¼ inch apart on a baking sheet lined with parchment paper. Bake the crackers until lightly browned, 10 to 12 minutes. Transfer to a rack to cool. Store crackers in an airtight container up to 2 weeks.

SPICY BEER BRITTLE

(Fills 1 [12 x 17-Inch] sheet pan)

2 cups sugar

1 cup light corn syrup

1 cup flat, room temperature Cape Cod Red Ale, or another amber ale

2 cups shelled raw or roasted peanuts

¼ teaspoon salt, if using raw peanuts

⅛ teaspoon chipotle chili powder, optional

1 tablespoon butter

1 teaspoon baking soda

1 teaspoon vanilla

Coat a rimmed baking sheet with butter or nonstick cooking spray. Combine the sugar, corn syrup, and beer in a large saucepan. Attach a candy thermometer to the side of the pan and place the pan over medium heat. Stir continuously until sugar is completely dissolved. When mixture comes to a boil, watch closely until thermometer registers 245°F (soft ball stage).

Add peanuts (plus salt if using raw nuts) and chipotle chili powder and continue to cook until thermometer registers 300°F. Remove from heat and quickly add the butter, baking soda, and vanilla, stirring until evenly blended. Return to stove and cook 1 to 2 minutes more.

Remove from heat and immediately scrape the hot brittle onto the prepared baking sheet, spreading with a wooden spoon. Cool completely, then break into pieces. Store in an airtight container at room temperature up to 1 month.

Cape Cod Central Dinner Train

While writing this book I talked to chefs about food, their cooking, and their experiences. But it was Chef Richard Davis who had the most unusual chef's job. He cooks on a moving train. He told me it is a very unique experience. "You have to go with the flow (in more than one respect) because of the motion of the train," he says. "It adds another element to cooking." According to Chef Davis everything is a matter of timing and, especially, balance. "My feet and legs have to be in the right position every minute while the train is moving. When I slice the tenderloin, my balance is extremely important because, if it isn't, I could slice off my hand."

Chef Davis has had his own business for twenty-eight years and has been a subcontractor for the railroad for seventeen years. He does all the food and beverages. The kitchen area in the train is extremely small. "You have the bar with drinks, the small dishwashing area, pots, pans, silverware, linens, and tableware. Orchestration in sequence and timing is critical," he explains. He also says that in the restaurant business it is important to have a good team. "You are only as good as your team. With a good team you win the game. Some of the people I work with have been here as long as I have. On Thanksgiving we did 220 dinners! It's kind of fun to work the train."

The train serves lunch and dinner. Board the lunch train in Hyannis at noon, or hop on the dinner train at six in the evening. The ride for dinner is about three hours. You can also have Sunday brunch on the train. That trip leaves Hyannis at eleven and comes back at one. The Central Dinner Train also offers a special Murder Mystery Dinner trip, a Taste of Italy trip, and a

New Year's Gala. During the day the train goes along the Cape Cod Canal, where you can watch people biking on the service road and see boats in the canal. At night the lights of the passing towns flicker in the windows as you speed along the Cape. It's an experience not to be missed!

252 Main Street, Hyannis, MA 02601, (508) 771-3800, capetrain.com

BREAST OF CHICKEN HOMMARDE

(Serves 2)

FOR CHICKEN:

¼ cup all-purpose flour
½ teaspoon salt
½ teaspoon freshly cracked
    black pepper
1 extra large egg, beaten well
½ teaspoon fresh chopped dill
3 tablespoons olive oil
2 chicken breasts

FOR LOBSTER BEURRE BLANC:

1 stick butter
1 medium shallot, minced
¼ cup white wine
¼ cup heavy cream
Juice of 1 lemon
2 ounces fresh cooked lobster
    meat, cut into pieces

Preheat oven to 350°F.

For the chicken: Combine the flour, salt, and pepper in a shallow bowl. Combine the egg and dill in another shallow bowl; beat well to blend.

Heat the olive oil in a medium-size saucepan. Dredge the chicken breast in the flour, shaking off any excess; coat with the egg mixture letting the excess drip back in the bowl before carefully laying the chicken in the hot pan. Cook until brown on both sides 1 to 2 minutes per side. Transfer the chicken to a baking sheet and place in the oven to finish cooking, about 15 minutes.

For the Lobster Beurre Blanc: While the chicken is in the oven, return the sauté pan to medium heat and add 1 tablespoon of the butter. Add the shallot and sauté until translucent about 5 minutes. Add the wine and heavy cream and simmer until reduced and thickened. Remove pan from heat and gradually whisk in the remaining butter. Add the lobster meat and mix well.

To plate: Place the chicken breasts on two serving plates, top each with lobster meat, and divide the Beurre Blanc between the two portions.

Centerville Pie Company

Laurie Bowen's signature chicken pot pie had been very popular among family and friends. In fact it became so popular and the demand became so great that she and friend Kristin Broadley decided to make a business of it. In 2009 they realized a long-held dream when they opened their own restaurant and pie company. The Centerville Pie Company opened in March of that year, and since then Laurie and Kristin have been known as "the Pie Ladies."

But that's only part of the story. In August 2009 Oprah Winfrey was on the Cape for Eunice Kennedy Shriver's funeral. Kristin found out where she was staying and dropped off one of those chicken pot pies. Oprah fell in love with this savory comfort food. From then on it was "the Oprah Factor." She had the Pie Ladies on her program and at the end of the year, even added the Centerville Pie Company to her list of Ultimate Favorite Things. Business started to boom into the national market. A bigger kitchen and more production space became necessary. Then an arrangement was made with Cape Abilities, a nearby nonprofit organization that provides jobs and services for people with disabilities across Cape Cod. Now much of the pie-making operation is handled by Cape Abilities. Laurie and Kristin donate a portion of their proceeds to the organization.

The Centerville Pie Company makes a variety of delicious pies. Popular fruit pies include traditional apple pie and local favorite cranapple pie, or there are savory pies like the Braised Beef Pie made with the Cape Cod Beer Company's Porter Beer.

1671 Falmouth Road, Centerville, MA 02632, (774) 470-1406, centervillepies.com

CENTERVILLE PIE COMPANY APPLE PIE

(Serves 8)

FOR THE CRUST:

All-purpose flour for rolling out
  dough
1 double recipe of your favorite
  pie dough

FOR THE FILLING:

⅓ cup sugar
3 tablespoons all-purpose flour
¾ teaspoon cinnamon
½ teaspoon ground nutmeg
6 medium Granny Smith apples
  (about 3 pounds), cored and
  sliced
1 tablespoon fresh lemon juice
2 tablespoons unsalted butter,
  cut into small pieces
Enough milk to brush top crust

For the crust: On a lightly floured work surface, roll out the pie dough to form two 11-inch circles. Fit one of the circles into a 9-inch pie pan, trimming to a 1½-inch overhang. Cover the second circle of dough with a dry towel while you prepare the filling.

For the filling: Preheat oven to 425°F. Combine the sugar, flour, cinnamon, and nutmeg in a large bowl and mix well. Add the apples and toss until apples are evenly coated with the sugar mixture. Add the lemon juice and toss again.

Pile the apples into the pie shell and dot with butter. Brush the rim of the pie shell with water just to moisten. Gently center the second circle of dough over the apples, pressing lightly around the rim so the moistened edge adheres slightly. Trim away the excess edge from the top crust and bring the overhanging edge of the bottom crust up and over the trimmed edge to seal. Crimp the edges of the pie decoratively with your fingers or with the tines of a fork. Cut a few slits in the center of the crust to release steam and brush with a little milk.

Place the pie on a baking sheet and bake 15 to 20 minutes. Reduce oven temperature to 350°F, and continue baking until the crust is lightly browned and the apples are tender when poked through the slits, 25 to 30 minutes more. Serve warm or cold.

Cranberry Bog Harvest

Each fall, sometime between October and November, you can drive around Cape Cod and see cranberries being harvested. It is spectacular to witness the red sea of cranberries against a backdrop of blue water, sky, and fall foliage. The harvest starts with the flooding of the bogs where cranberries grow. This happens for a day or so, and then the actual harvest begins. In the beginning the cranberries were harvested by laborers with scoops (see photo of old scoop, at right). Today the berries are usually corralled and contained in a selected area then harvested by machine and loaded onto trucks.

The cranberry is found only in the northern part of the country. Native Americans discovered the cranberry first; they used them as food, as a healing agent, and also for a dye. When the Pilgrims arrived, they called the red berries craneberry because the pink blossoms that appear in the spring resembled the head and bill of the Sandhill crane.

The Cape Cod Cranberry Growers' Association was established in 1888. It is one of the oldest farmers organizations in the country. Visit their website at cranberries.com to find recipes, harvest celebrations, and more.

Cranberry Bog Harvest Recipes

CRANBERRY CHUTNEY

Chutney has a variety of uses. Try a piece of cheese on a cracker topped with a dollop of chutney, or use chutney as the perfect accompaniment to boiled meats. This recipe was adapted from *The Green Briar Jam Kitchen Cookbook* (see Jam Kitchen, page 48).

(Yield: 5–6 Pint jars)

1 pound fresh cranberries, picked over

¾ pound Granny Smith apples, peeled, cored, and chopped

1 medium onion, peeled and chopped

1 cup brown sugar

½ cup raisins

½ cup cider vinegar

½ cup water

¼ cup candied ginger

½ minced lemon

½ teaspoon chili powder

½ teaspoon dry mustard

½ teaspoon kosher salt

Combine all ingredients in a large kettle and mix well. Bring to a boil, reduce heat, and cook until thick, about 1 hour or more, skimming the foam from the surface. Pour into 8-ounce sterilized jars and seal.

CRANBERRY NUT BREAD

Claire Desilets (see Cranberry Bog Honey, page 118) uses honey for anything calling for sugar. Here is one of her recipes for a delicious bread, perfect for that afternoon tea break.

(Makes 2 loaves)

2 large eggs, room temperature

1⅓ cups orange juice, room temperature

¾ cup honey

¾ cup brown sugar

½ cup unsalted butter, melted

2 tablespoons freshly grated orange zest

5 cups flour

1 tablespoon baking powder

1 teaspoon baking soda

1 teaspoon salt

3–4 cups fresh cranberries, coarsely chopped

½ cup chopped walnuts

Butter two 9 x 5 x 3-inch loaf pans and set aside. Place the eggs in a large mixing bowl and beat well. Add the orange juice, honey, brown sugar, melted butter, and orange zest. Whisk or stir until thoroughly blended.

In another bowl, sift together the flour, baking powder, baking soda, and salt; add to the wet ingredients, stirring just until combined. Fold in the cranberries and nuts, and divide the batter between the pans.

Preheat oven to 350°F, allowing the batter to rest 20 minutes as the oven comes up to temperature. Bake the loaves until a tester comes out clean and tops are browned, about 50 to 55 minutes. Allow loaves to cool in pans 25 to 30 minutes. Turn out onto a wire rack and cool at least 30 minutes more before slicing.

I first met Martha Kane when she was the chef at the Brewster Fish House. I followed her to her own restaurant on Main Street in Dennis Village. The building next to the famous Cape Playhouse and Cape Cinema was extensively renovated by Martha's husband, Jonathan Smith, a Brewster native, carpenter, fisherman, and oyster farmer. FIN opened in March 2011. The rooms in this two-story building are cozy and warm. The side door leads you directly into the bar, which is small but comfortable. If you choose to dine at the bar, you will probably have Tina as your server. If that is the case, you will be well taken care of. There are two dining rooms, one downstairs and one upstairs. Each provides the perfect setting to experience Martha's focus on local contemporary seafood dishes.

Over the years Martha has cultivated relationships with local farmers and fishermen. She does most of her sourcing close to home and takes to heart the "Buy Local Buy Fresh" concept. When I asked her how she got into the restaurant business, she told me that she originally went to school to be an artist and has a Bachelor of Fine Arts degree. "I worked my way through school by working in restaurants. It was there that the interest in food happened. I now incorporate and combine my art background into my food." This is obvious when you think about her concept and presentation of the items on the menu, which are creative and innovative yet not overly complicated. And her food is delicious. Try the house made oyster chowder (made with Jonathan's oysters), the seared native flounder, or her organic grass-fed beef (recipe opposite) and you'll understand.

800 Main Street, Dennis, MA 02638, (508) 385-2096, fincapecod.com

GRILLED PINELAND FARMS RIB EYE STEAK

It was mid-February, a week after Valentine's Day, and we decided to go to FIN. The Rib Eye Steak was on the menu but a different version of what Martha did in this recipe. We ordered it and here is what she did: Yukon gold potato puree, caramelized shallots, which were sprinkled over the potatoes, wilted watercress and a red wine jus, not on the meat but a gentle pool elegantly designed around the inside of the plate. Wonderfully satisfying for a cold winter night! There are many parts to Chef Kane's recipe. You may choose to do the whole recipe but you also can choose to take sections and add them to a dinner you are creating. For example, make the garlic chips and place them over a piece of fish or chicken, use the vinaigrette for your salad or the fingerling potatoes as a side dish. Think creatively when it comes to the chef's recipes.

(Serves 4)

FOR THE GARLIC CHIPS:
12 garlic cloves, sliced as thinly as possible
Milk
Canola oil for frying

FOR THE VINAIGRETTE:
1 cup veal demi-glace, warmed (optional)
¼ cup extra-virgin olive oil
2 tablespoons champagne vinegar
1 tablespoon freshly cracked black pepper
1 teaspoon kosher salt

For the garlic chips: Place the garlic slices in a small saucepan and add enough milk to just cover the slices. Bring to a boil, then drain off the milk, leaving the garlic in the pan. Add enough fresh milk to cover the slices again; bring to a boil. Drain, rinse, and pat dry. Preheat the oil in a small deep fryer or cast iron skillet to 300°F. Fry the garlic slices until slightly browned and crispy. Drain well on paper towels and season with salt. Set aside until serving time.

For the vinaigrette: Whisk the demi-glace (if using), oil, vinegar, pepper, and salt together in a small bowl. Set aside until serving time.

For the potato salad: Place the potatoes in a large saucepan and add water to cover by at least an inch. Bring to a boil over high heat; cook until potatoes are just tender when tested with a paring knife, about 10 minutes. Drain well. When the potatoes are cool enough to handle, slice in half and place in a large mixing bowl; refrigerate until cold.

Meanwhile, place the bacon in a sauté pan over medium-low heat and cook, stirring occasionally, until the bacon renders some of its fat and turns crisp and brown. Using a slotted spoon, transfer the bacon to paper towels to drain.

Place the corn over a medium-hot grill and cook, turning occasionally, until golden brown and lightly charred in spots. Transfer the corn to a cutting board; maintain the grill temperature to cook the steaks. When cool enough to handle, cut the kernels from the cobs; there should be about 2 cups. Add the bacon and corn to the chilled potatoes, along with the scallions and chives, and toss gently to combine.

In a small bowl, whisk together the mayonnaise, mascarpone, harissa, and lemon juice. Add the dressing to the potatoes and mix gently until thoroughly combined. Season with salt and freshly ground white pepper to taste. Cover and refrigerate until serving time.

For the steaks: Season both sides of the steaks with salt and pepper and grill over a medium-hot fire. Transfer to a platter and tent loosely with foil.

To assemble the dish: Place the arugula in a large mixing bowl. Whisk the oil and lemon juice together in a small bowl and season with salt and pepper. Toss the dressing with the arugula; set aside. Slice each steak and arrange on four dinner plates with potato salad on the side. Whisk the vinaigrette to blend and spoon some over each dish. Top with arugula and garlic chips.

FOR THE POTATO SALAD:
1 pound fingerling potatoes, scrubbed
2 thick slices applewood smoked bacon, diced
4 ears fresh corn, shucked and silks removed
4 scallions, thinly sliced on the bias
2 tablespoons minced fresh chives
½ cup mayonnaise
2 tablespoons mascarpone cheese
1 tablespoon harissa (or other hot chile paste)
1 tablespoon fresh lemon juice
Salt to taste
Freshly ground white pepper to taste

FOR THE STEAKS:
4 (8-ounce) Pineland Farms rib eye steaks
Kosher salt and cracked black pepper to taste

4 cups baby arugula
2 tablespoons extra-virgin olive oil
2 tablespoons fresh lemon juice
Salt and pepper to taste

LEMON TART WITH FRESH BERRIES

(Makes 8 individual tarts)

FOR THE TART DOUGH:

1½ cups (12 ounces or 3 sticks)
    unsalted butter, slightly
    softened
¾ cup sugar
1 egg
2 teaspoons vanilla extract
3 cups all-purpose flour
1 teaspoon salt

FOR THE LEMON CURD:

4 eggs
4 egg yolks
¾ cup sugar
¾ cup fresh lemon juice (from
    3–4 lemons)
4 tablespoons (2 ounces) cold
    unsalted butter, cut in pieces
Fresh seasonal berries, washed
    and patted dry

For the tart dough: Cream the butter and sugar together in the bowl of a standing electric mixer until light and fluffy. Add the egg and vanilla; beat until completely incorporated. Gradually add the flour and salt, mixing until the dough forms a ball. Divide the dough in half and wrap each half in plastic wrap. Refrigerate 15 minutes.

Roll out half of the dough on a lightly floured work surface to ¼-inch thickness. Cut four circles from the dough, each 5 inches in diameter, and fit them into four 4½-inch tart pans with removable bottoms. Repeat with the remaining dough to make 4 more tart shells. Place the tarts on a baking sheet and refrigerate until firm, 10 to 15 minutes. Preheat oven to 350°F. Bake the tart shells on the baking sheet until golden brown, 15 to 20 minutes. Cool tart shells completely before removing from the pans.

For the lemon curd: Whisk together the eggs, egg yolks, and sugar in a shallow stainless steel bowl until sugar dissolves. Add the lemon juice, mix well, and place the bowl over a saucepan of simmering water. (The bowl should not touch the water.) Whisk constantly until the mixture thickens and wisps of steam just begin to rise; do not overcook or the eggs will curdle. Remove the bowl from heat and whisk in the butter. Strain the curd into a clean bowl, press plastic wrap against the surface, and vent the plastic wrap in several places with the point of a knife. Refrigerate until cold.

To assemble the dish: Place each tart shell on a dessert plate and neatly spoon some lemon curd into each one. Decorate artfully with berries. This desert is the creation of the pastry chef at FIN, Cristine Arden.

Christine Arden, the pastry chef at FIN, puts the finishing touches on her prize lemon tart.

Four Seas Ice Cream

What is a summer vacation on a hot summer evening without a dripping cone of your favorite ice cream? And where is the best place to get that cone? Anyone vacationing on Cape Cod between May and September knows that a trip to Four Seas Ice Cream on a warm summer night is a must. Order your cone or a sundae, stand outside the store with the locals and other vacationers, and enjoy.

The character, look, and feel of Four Seas has been the same for decades. Once a blacksmith shop, it is now quintessential old Cape Cod. The original wood floors slant, and on the walls are old 4 SEAS license plates, framed group pictures of high school students who've worked in the shop, and the original black pegboards with the ice cream flavors that are available—or not—that day. The ice cream is homemade, and the selection is filled with old favorites: black raspberry, cookie dough, peanut butter chocolate chip, frozen pudding, pistachio, coconut, ginger, and coffee. Make sure you try their famous peach ice cream. This is the ice cream that Jackie Kennedy Onassis ordered for daughter Caroline's wedding.

During lunchtime grab a Four Seas sandwich. The lobster salad is popular, but you can also find peanut butter and jelly, cream cheese and olive, egg salad, ham and cheese, and other classic selections.

This famous Cape Cod institution in Centerville was founded in 1934 and got its name from the original owner, W. Wells Watson. The "Four Seas" are the four bodies of water that surround the Cape: the Atlantic Ocean, Buzzards Bay, Cape Cod Bay, and Nantucket Sound. In 1960 Dick Warren, a Barnstable High school teacher, bought the shop and operated it until 2001, when he sold it to his son and daughter-in-law, Doug and Peggy. Make sure to stop by this Cape Cod tradition.

360 South Main Street, Centerville, MA 02632, (508) 775-1394, fourseasicecream.com

PEACH ICE CREAM

(Makes about 1 quart)

FOR THE FRUIT:

1 pound (about 3 medium large) fresh ripe peaches, washed and pitted

1¼ cups sugar, divided

1 tablespoon fresh lemon juice

¼ teaspoon almond extract

FOR THE CUSTARD:

1 cup whole milk

3 egg yolks

2 cups heavy cream

For the fruit: Slice the peaches with the skin on; they should yield about 2 cups. Place peaches in a food processor along with ¼ cup sugar, lemon juice, and almond extract. Pulse 8 to 10 times to chop the peaches, leaving some small chunks. Set aside.

For the custard: Place about 1 cup ice cubes in a shallow metal bowl and place another metal bowl on top. Rest a fine sieve in the top bowl, and set aside. In the top of a double boiler, whisk the remaining 1 cup sugar, milk, and egg yolks until frothy. Place the pan over simmering water and cook, stirring constantly, until the mixture thickens enough to coat the back of a spoon and wisps of steam begin to form, 10 to 15 minutes. (Do not let the mixture boil or it will curdle.) Remove from heat and strain the custard into a bowl. Stir in the heavy cream, cover the custard bowl with plastic wrap, and refrigerate until very cold, 4 to 24 hours.

To assemble the dish: Pour the custard into an ice cream maker and freeze according to the manufacturer's directions. Halfway through the churning process, add the peaches and continue to churn as directed. Transfer to a freezer container; the ice cream will be very soft. Place the container in the freezer for 2 to 4 hours to firm up before serving.

Happy Fish Bakery

Self-taught, Emily Burbank bakes some of the most delicious pastries and breads on the Cape at the Happy Fish Bakery. The bakery is housed in a beautifully renovated old building on historic Route 6A. Here you will find an artist creating some unique takes on traditional European treats.

Walking into the main floor of the bakery, you immediately feel a sense of quality, refinement, and taste, both in the products and style of the room. Directly in front is the main counter filled with beautiful pastries and breads. There are Emily's French croissants (plain, almond, and chocolate), sticky buns, and round boules of rye and white. Another unusual item, not often found on Cape Cod, is her take on the beautiful panettone, the traditional Italian Christmas bread. This is the perfect year-round gift (it comes in two sizes), for anyone, and not only at Christmas. To the left of the counter is a small room with a few small tables and chairs to have coffee or tea, and relax with one of the delicious pastries.

173 Route 6A, Yarmouth, MA 02675, (774) 994-8272

Good Butter Bakery

Terri always felt at home in the kitchen with either her grandmother making bread or her mother making chocolate chip cookies. Later in life she worked with the famous artisanal bread baker Mark Furstenberg in Washington, DC. "He was a big influence in my life, and I was able to get scholarships to study in Paris."

I first met Terri at local farmers' markets selling her now-famous Kayak Cookies. Terri's cookies started in Washington, DC, where she lived and worked as a pastry chef. In 1979 she gave up working as a pastry chef and dedicated herself full-time to making her salty oats homemade Kayak Cookies. They were a big hit, and the sale of the cookies took off in the nation's capital. Then in 2005 she moved to the Cape. "When I was a child, we came here for summers because my family had a place here," Terri says. "I love the sea, ocean, and outdoors and decided to move here and start a business." This is the dream of most people who summer and vacation on Cape Cod, but most do not last through that first winter.

Terri designed her bakery as a large, open industrial space. It is fairly sparse but was done with impeccable taste. Terri is a perfectionist and is dedicated to the quality of her product.

"My real thing is working with dough. It is so tactile. I love the texture and could roll out dough all day long." At the time of this writing, Terri makes some special-order-only items. I asked Terri what her favorite are, "My specialty is anything with butter!" she says.

239 Main Street (around the corner on Pleasant), Hyannis, MA 02601, (508) 827-7353

BRIOCHE ROASTED RHUBARB BREAD PUDDING

(Serves 8)

1 loaf brioche, crusts removed
   and cubed
1¼ cups roasted rhubarb (cut
   into ¾-inch pieces)
1 vanilla bean
6 cups heavy cream
8 large eggs
1¼ cups sugar

Butter an 8- x 12-inch baking dish and fill with brioche cubes and roasted rhubarb. Set aside.

Scrape the seeds of the vanilla bean into a saucepan with the cream and add the bean itself. Heat cream to a boil, remove from heat, and let sit for 5 minutes to infuse the vanilla into the cream.

In a mixing bowl, whisk together the eggs and sugar until well combined. Gently pour the hot cream into the egg mixture, whisking as you go. Strain and pour the mixture over the brioche-filled baking pan.

Preheat oven to 325°F. Put the baking dish in a large pan (a roasting pan works well), place pan in the oven, and pour boiling water into the pan until it reaches halfway up the sides of the baking dish. Bake until the custard is set, about 40 to 45 minutes; test for doneness with a small sharp knife. Remove from oven and let cool.

Refrigerate bread pudding if not eating the same day. Serve with Strawberry Rhubarb Butter Sauce (below).

STRAWBERRY RHUBARB BUTTER SAUCE

(Makes about 3 cups)

2 cups strawberries, sliced
1 cup chopped rhubarb
¾–1 cup sugar, depending on the
   ripeness of the strawberries
½ vanilla bean, scraped
½ teaspoon lemon juice
2 tablespoons butter

Combine all ingredients except butter in a saucepan and cook just until sugar is dissolved and mixture begins to bubble.

Remove from heat and stir in the butter. Strain and chill.

ROSEMARY BREAD STICKS

(Makes 2 dozen bread sticks)

1 cup plus 2 tablespoons
  lukewarm water
1¾ teaspoons dry yeast
5 tablespoons extra-virgin olive
  oil
3½ tablespoons soft butter
4 cups flour
2 teaspoons sea salt
8 tablespoons chopped rosemary

Put the water in a medium-size bowl and add the yeast. Let rest for 5 minutes.

Add the rest of the ingredients, except the rosemary. Mix until the flour is almost incorporated. Put dough onto lightly floured surface and knead for about 5 to 7 minutes. If dough is sticky to touch, add a few tablespoons of flour, a little at a time, to create a firm dough. Make a ball with the dough and place in a warm, lightly oiled bowl; cover and let rest in a warm place for 1 hour.

Place risen dough on lightly floured surface and gently stretch into a rectangular shape. Divide the dough into about 1¼-ounce portions and place on a large surface or a sheet pan. Cover with plastic wrap and let rest for 15 minutes.

Roll out each piece to about 15 inches long. Before placing on a sheet pan, bread sticks can be rolled in semolina and/or sea salt and rosemary. Bread sticks are ready to bake after rolling.

Bake bread sticks at 375°F for about 20 minutes or until golden brown.

The Local Juice

I met Nicole Cormier in a restaurant one night; we chatted and exchanged cards. We did not see each other for several years. Occasionally I would hear her radio program on WOMR. I finally got the scope of her passion when I went into The Local Juice. Nicole is a Registered Dietitian, and Jen Villa is an artist and owner of The Little Beach Gallery next door. They both have a deep passion and love for local sustainability, community advocacy, and health and wellness. In March 2014, they decided to join forces selling their local cold-pressed juices locally.

In July 2016 they opened The Local Juice in Hyannis. In addition to offering their signature, cold-pressed juices in pleasant indoor and outdoor settings, they also sell smoothies to go, Snowy Owl Coffee, and local farm products including fresh eggs, honey, hot sauces, chocolate, produce, and much more. It is a fun place to get juiced!

539 South Street, Hyannis, MA 02601, (508) 775-5552, TheLocalJuice.Com

ENERGY BURSTS

(Makes about 30)

These colorful balls make a great snack or addition to your meal; they are loaded with vitamins and protein.

4 cups shredded carrots
1 cup ground almonds
1 cup pumpkin seeds (pepitas)
1 cup chia seeds
1 cup dried goji berries
1 cup dried mulberries
1 cup shredded unsweetened
    coconut
1 cup maple syrup
6 dried dates, pitted

Combine everything in a food processor (you may have to divide the batch, depending on the size of your food processor). Blend for 30-90 seconds, until the nuts are chopped (you can alter this depending on how fine or chunky you'd like your batter). Remove from the processor and place in a bowl. Chill the batter in the fridge for 15-30 minutes. Roll small pieces of batter into balls the size of a golf ball (you can vary this, too). They will keep in the fridge for about a week. Enjoy!

Cape Cod Cottage Industries

Cape Cod Cranberry Bog Honey

Claire and Paul Desilets, farmfresh.org

Claire, an East Sandwich resident since 1948, was raised in an active 4-H family who lived adjacent to cranberry bogs. She kept bees as a 4-H project, graduated from Sandwich High School, and then went to college. That's where she met Paul, who was from Fall River, a city along the Massachusetts–Rhode Island border. They each have a degree in pharmacology. Claire and Paul married and settled in East Sandwich. Paul passed away three years ago and Clair now managers over fifty hives on cranberry bogs that have been family-owned since the late 1980s.

Clair is a member of the Barnstable County Beekeepers Association where she has held many positions of leadership. They instruct new beekeepers in the art and enjoyment of beekeeping on Cape Cod. When anyone mentions beekeeping on Cape Cod, Desilet is the first name that come to mind.

Cape Cod Cranberry Harvest Jams, Jellies, and Preserves

Debbie Greiner and Tina Labossiere, cranberryharvest.com

Their story began in 1995 at a children's play group, where Debbie and Tina became instant friends and, soon after that, great business partners. They started out making Ballerina Bunnies, but when an acquaintance suggested they make a food product,

Debbie and Tina created their first homemade cranberry jelly. Now, eight children and many jelly flavors later, they are still friends, still cooking, and the proud proprietors of Cape Cod Cranberry Harvest. It has been an incredible journey for Debbie and Tina, and they look forward to many more years of friendship and jelly-making together.

Cape Cod Potato Chips

Lynn and Steve Bernard, capecodchips.com

Something that started out as a small cottage industry on Cape Cod has turned into a national success. Founded in 1980 by Lynn and Steve Bernard with no knowledge of the snack food business, Cape Cod Potato Chips has become

a local institution and one of the biggest tourist attractions on the Cape. Steve originally owned an auto parts business. He purchased a potato slicer for three thousand dollars, and he and Lynn began making kettle-cooked chips in their kitchen. Over thirty years later they have developed many varieties of chips. They moved from the kitchen to a small storefront and then to the factory located at 100 Breed's Hill Road in Hyannis. Tours are given Monday through Friday from nine to five.

Cape Cod Saltworks

Janice Burling and Penny Lewis

Saltworks on Cape Cod date back to the 1800s. At that time much of the Cape's industries revolved around fishing, whaling, and agriculture. As the fishing industry grew, salt became the best way to preserve fish and saltworks sprang up in many towns on the Cape.

Today refrigeration has replaced salt, but the tradition of salt making is being carried on by Cape Cod Saltworks. Janice Burling and Penny Lewis started this venture in their home and have now moved their operation to Cape Abilities Farm in Dennis. This artisanal, 100 percent, all-natural salt has no additives and is evaporated from the waters of Barnstable Harbor and Nauset Beach in Orleans. It can be purchased from specialty shops around the Cape.

Just Jars

Judy Fratus, Program Coordinator, jfratus@monomoy.edu

Just Jars takes mixes for breads, cookies, and soup, puts them in mason jars with fabric-covered lids and attached recipes. These cleverly packaged jars are produced in the Chatham High School Special Needs Vocational program. Just Jars can be found in the Dennis Cape Abilities Farm Shop and the Cape Abilities Farm to Table Shop, which is located in Chatham's Historical District on the road to the Chatham Lighthouse. The shop is also staffed by students from Chatham High School and carries other local products.

Grin Hola Premium Granola

Jason Warren, Grinhola.Com

Jason Warren owned the Osterville Village Café for over 3 years and during that time, he made his granola for his clients—the more he made, the more he sold. In 2014 Warren sold the café to Amie Smith (now Amie's Bakery). I met Jason at a local farmers' market where he was selling his granola. I bought the original, Maple Cranberry; it is one of the best granolas around. Today Jason divides his time between baking, packing, and delivering his prized six granola flavors to local stores on Cape Cod.

COCA NUTTY MARSHMALLOW BARS

This is a recipe Warren developed around his Coca Nutty Granola.

1 (3 cups) full package of Coca Nutty Granola

2 tablespoons butter

5 ounces marshmallows (half of a 10-ounce package)

Melt butter in a large saucepan over low heat. Add marshmallows and stir until melted and well blended. Remove from heat. Add granola and stir until well combined. Using a buttered spatula, press mixture evenly and firmly into an 8 x 8-inch square pan, which has been lined with buttered parchment paper. Cool for an hour or more before cutting into 2 x 2 inch squares.

Naked Oyster Raw Bistro and Bar

Owner and executive chef Florence Lowell has been in the restaurant business for some time. "For the past thirty years I have spent most of that time in the restaurant business. I lived in Austin and Houston before moving to Cape Cod eight years ago," she says. Five years ago she and her husband, David, bought an oyster grant in Barnstable Harbor. Florence grew up close to the Atlantic Coast of France, near Bordeaux, and spent summers in Arcachon, a major oyster-farming center. Becoming an oyster farmer strengthened her commitment to using local ingredients and brought back childhood memories. "It all made sense; now I could supply my own restaurant with these local, extremely fresh, tasty, and delicious oysters!"

When Florence and I spoke, she told me, "At this moment we have over three thousand oysters. Some of them are ready for market and the rest will be ready next year." Farming oysters is a delicate process, but the payoff is obvious in the restaurant's menu. After making your selection from the varied menu, you can choose to dine inside or, during the summer months, outside for people watching.

Florence's son Julien is now a chef in the restaurant. He's been working in restaurants since he was eleven, peeling vegetables at his father's Houston restaurant. "I spent a year in France at Biarritz at a culinary school in southern France near the Spain border," he says. He's twenty-six now and has been living on Cape Cod for four years. He's fluent in French, and, like his mother, has a passion for cooking. His Oyster Stew (see page 127) is a rich, wonderful treat!

410 Main Street (Pearl Street), Hyannis, MA 02601, (508) 778-6500, nakedoyster.com

CLAM CHOWDER
(Serves 6–8)

⅓ cup unsalted butter
1 large Spanish onion, peeled
　　and diced
2 celery stalks, sliced
½ cup all-purpose flour
4 cups clam juice (or part
　　chicken broth or seafood
　　stock)
1½ cups light cream
2–3 cups peeled, diced potatoes
1 tablespoon fresh thyme leaves
2–3 cups chopped sea clams
Sea salt and freshly ground
　　pepper to taste

Melt butter in a pot over medium heat. Add the onion and celery and sauté until onion is translucent, about 8 minutes. Gradually whisk in the flour and continue cooking and stirring until no white flour remains and mixture just begins to color, about 2 minutes. Gradually whisk in the clam juice, stirring constantly to keep the mixture smooth, and bring to a boil. Add the cream and simmer until slightly thickened, stirring occasionally. Add the potatoes and thyme and simmer until potatoes are just tender, about 8 minutes. Stir in the clams, return to a simmer, and cook just until the clams are opaque, about 1 minute more. Remove from heat. Season with sea salt and freshly ground black pepper to taste.

OYSTER STEW

Author's Nore: Good Butter Bakery's Rosemary Bread Sticks (page 115) would be wonderful served alongside this stew.

(Serves 4)

FOR THE STEW:

1 tablespoon light olive oil

¼ cup minced shallots

2 tablespoons brandy

½ cup sherry

4 cups heavy cream

24 fresh oysters, shucked, juice reserved

Salt and pepper to taste

¼ cup minced chives or chopped parsley for garnish

For the stew: Heat the oil in a 2-quart, straight-sided sauté pan over medium-high heat. Add the shallots and cook until translucent, about 4 minutes. Add the brandy and quickly, carefully wave a long lit match just above the surface to light it. When the flame dies down, add the sherry, simmering to reduce the sherry slightly. Add the cream, bring to a boil, and reduce by half. Add the oysters with their juices and poach for 45 seconds; do not overcook. Season with salt and pepper.

To assemble the dish: Divide the stew evenly among four warm bowls, garnish with chives, and serve immediately.

Pizza Barbone

Jason O'Toole grew up on the Cape in Falmouth and has been working in restaurants since he was seventeen years old. O'Toole studied at the Culinary Institute of America in New York and worked with Chef Gordon Ramsey of reality television fame in London. After London he returned to Massachusetts and worked in the Boston area before returning to Cape Cod to start his own catering business.

The catering went well, but the real adventure started in 2010 when Jason attached a mobile wood-fired oven to the back of his catering van and Pizza Barbone was born. "We were hitting the farmers' markets, catering special events and public and private parties from Cape Cod to Boston and becoming well-known for our pizzas," says Jason. Things were going well but Jason wanted something more. "I have always had the dream of opening my own restaurant, centered around my pizzas," he says, and in 2012 Pizza Barbone arrived on Main Street in Hyannis. Because his catering and mobile pizza business was so successful, he kept the name Barbone, which in Italian means "tramp" or "vagabond."

The restaurant is simply designed; for seating Jason found and refinished some pews from a little church in northern Massachusetts. But the real showpiece is the Stefano Ferrara wood-fired oven that you can see from every seat in the restaurant. "It is made from rock and ash from Mt. Vesuvius, the volcano in Southern Italy. Stefano Ferrara is a builder of handmade firewood ovens in Naples, Italy," explains Jason. "It is a functional piece of art and weighs over six thousand pounds. There are only twenty-five in the United States, and I have the only one in Massachusetts."

390 Main Street, Hyannis, MA 02601, (508) 957-2377, pizzabarbone.com

PIZZA DOUGH

For his pizzas, Chef Jason O'Toole uses flour imported from Antico Molino Caputo from Naples, Italy. Caputo flour is blended to have a far lower protein content, which allows the dough to stretch out and keep its shape much better than the all-purpose flour we are used to. It is also formulated specifically for high-heat baking. Caputo has been using this well-kept secret formula since 1924. The "Tipo 00" designation refers to the fineness of its grind. If Caputo flour is not available, make your own dough with regular flour or use a pre-made crust from your local grocery store.

(Makes 4 [12-inch] pizzas)

5 cups "Tipo 00" flour
2 cups plus 1 tablespoon warm water
1 teaspoon dried yeast
4 teaspoons kosher salt

Combine flour, water, and yeast in the bowl of an electric mixer fitted with a dough hook. Beat on low speed 2 minutes. Let rest for 20 minutes, then add salt. Beat dough again on low speed for 6 minutes; increase to medium speed and beat 2 minutes more.

Transfer dough to a floured work surface and divide into four equal-size balls. Fold each dough ball over itself to create a tight ball. Lightly dust a baking sheet with flour and place the dough balls on it, spaced well apart so they don't touch even when they spread. Cover with plastic wrap and refrigerate 24 to 48 hours, or freeze until ready to use.

Bring dough to room temperature before using. One at a time, transfer a dough ball to a floured work surface, working carefully to retain its round shape. With floured fingers, press the air from the dough, working from the center out to form a crust. Lightly pull and stretch the dough with floured hands into a 12-inch circle.

CORN & BACON PIZZA

(Makes 1 [12-inch] pizza)

1 unbaked 12-inch pizza crust
¼ cup cooked bacon
2 tablespoons roasted garlic
    puree
2 tablespoons caramelized onion
4 ounces fresh mozzarella, thinly
    sliced
1 ear of corn, kernels removed
1 teaspoon fresh thyme leaves
2 tablespoons freshly grated
    Parmesan cheese
Pinch salt

Preheat oven with a pizza stone to 500°F. Place the pizza crust on a lightly floured pizza peel. Spread roasted garlic puree and caramelized onion. Arrange mozzarella slices and distribute corn, bacon, and thyme evenly over the pizza. Sprinkle Parmesan cheese over and season with salt. Gently slide the pizza into the oven, on top of the preheated stone, and bake until crust is golden brown and puffy, 8 to 10 minutes.

MARGHERITA PIZZA

(Makes 1 [12-inch] pizza)

1 unbaked 12-inch pizza crust
¼ cup crushed tomatoes
4 ounces fresh mozzarella, thinly
    sliced
½ cup chopped fresh basil
3 tablespoons freshly grated
    Parmesan cheese
Pinch salt

Preheat oven with a pizza stone to 500°F. Place the pizza crust on a lightly floured pizza peel. Spread the crushed tomatoes on the dough, leaving a 1-inch border. Arrange the mozzarella slices on top of the tomatoes and scatter the basil on top. Sprinkle with Parmesan and a pinch of salt. Gently slide the pizza into the oven, on top of the preheated stone, and bake until crust is golden brown and puffy, 8 to 10 minutes.

SWEET SAUSAGE PIZZA

(Makes 1 [12-inch] pizza)

1 unbaked 12-inch pizza crust
¼ cup crushed tomatoes
3 ounces sweet sausage,
    casings removed, cooked,
    and crumbled
4 ounces fresh mozzarella, thinly
    sliced
½ small red onion, peeled and
    thinly sliced
1 tablespoon chopped fresh
    oregano
2 tablespoons freshly grated
    Parmesan cheese
Pinch salt

Preheat oven with a pizza stone to 500°F. Place the pizza crust on a lightly floured pizza peel. Spread crushed tomatoes on the dough, leaving a 1-inch border. Distribute crumbled sausage evenly over the sauce and arrange mozzarella slices on top. Scatter onions, oregano, and Parmesan over the cheese and season with salt. Gently slide the pizza into the oven, on top of the preheated stone, and bake until crust is golden brown and puffy, 8 to 10 minutes.

Vagabond Chef

When I first met French chef Yves Bainier, he was the chef at the Wianno Club in Osterville. He was also starting a business making and selling individual soufflés. I lost track of him until I had lunch at his new place, Vagabond Chef, in the old Big Al's Breakfast and Lunch diner. At Vagabond Chef that day, I not only had lunch, but went back for dinner to have one of his wagyu burgers with a homemade bun and ketchup!

At that time, Vagabond Chef was BYOB. The Colorado beef is all natural and comes from the finest 100% full-blooded Japanese cattle. The big specialty here are the burgers. They are topped with caramelized onions, lettuce, and tomato, plus a large portion of homemade, thinly sliced potato chips. Vagabond Chef also serves creative breakfasts.

1076 Route 6A, South Yarmouth, MA 02664, (508) 398-1960, Vagabondchefcc.com

LOWER CAPE

Atlantic Spice Company

Cape Cod is filled with unique and unexpected places to explore. The Atlantic Spice Company is one of them. If you are heading to Provincetown, veer off of Route 6, take a left onto Shore Road (6A), then take a sharp left up a small hill and you will be in spice heaven. The store has been around since 1994 and has over 450 different herbs and spices. You'll find specialty items like saffron, zahtar, and vanilla beans, along with any spice you might need to cook your favorite dish and any herbs you might need for herbal therapy. You cannot go into this store without buying a bag of something.

How can a spice company be so successful on Cape Cod? Linnet Hultin, Atlantic Spice's general manager, stays on top of the latest trends. Hultin is well versed in what sells. She has been with the store since it opened and trusts her instinct for finding new products. She skips trade shows and instead uses the latest cookbooks, recipes found online, newspapers, and magazines to find out what's hot and keep it in stock. And the store also has a large mail-order business that focuses on home cooks, chefs, specialty shops, and health food stores, both in and outside of the United States. "If it is a good seller in the store, then we add it to the wholesale business," she says.

There are other items in the store, such as colorful teapots, beautiful hand-crafted cutting boards, and interesting wooden and ceramic dishes that can be used for all kinds of things, from holding condiments at a dinner party to holding soap in a guest bath. If you have anyone

in your life who is difficult to buy a present for, I assure you that you'll find something at Atlantic Spice.

When I asked Linnet for a recipe, she said, "I want to use as many spices from the store as possible," and she came up with this delicious vegetarian curry.

2 Shore Road, North Truro, MA 02652, (800) 316-7965, atlanticspice.com

VEGETARIAN CURRY
(Serves 4)

FOR THE CURRY BASE:

3 tablespoons olive oil

1 large onion, peeled and chopped

2 medium carrots, peeled and diced

1½ tablespoons minced garlic cloves

1-inch piece fresh ginger, peeled and minced

1 tablespoon ground coriander

1 teaspoon ground cumin

1 teaspoon ground turmeric

½ teaspoon cayenne pepper

2 cups vegetable stock

1 (15.5-ounce) can unsweetened coconut milk

1 tablespoon tomato paste

1 (3-inch) cinnamon stick

FOR THE VEGETABLES:

2 large ripe tomatoes

1½ pounds cauliflower florets

1 pound sweet potatoes, peeled and diced (about 1¼ cups)

2 cups roughly chopped, washed, and dried fresh spinach leaves

1 (15.5 ounce) can chickpeas, rinsed and drained

1 lime, zested and juiced

Salt and pepper to taste

4 tablespoons fresh chopped cilantro (for garnish)

For the curry base: Heat oil in a large sauté pan or Dutch oven. Add the onion and carrots and cook over medium heat until onion is translucent, 5 to 7 minutes. Stir in garlic and ginger and cook for 1 minute more. Add the coriander, cumin, turmeric, and cayenne and cook 1 minute, stirring constantly. Add stock, coconut milk, tomato paste, and cinnamon stick and stir until evenly blended, about 1 minute. Raise the heat and bring to a boil, then adjust to a simmer and cook for 10 minutes until vegetables are tender.

For the vegetables: To skin the tomatoes, cut an X through just the skin on the bottom of each one and drop them into boiling water until skins loosen a bit, 20 to 60 seconds (riper tomatoes require less time). Transfer tomatoes to a bowl of ice water. One at a time, lift a tomato out of the water bath and slip off the skin. Chop the tomatoes and set aside.

Return the curry base to medium-high heat and add the tomatoes, cauliflower, and sweet potatoes, stirring to coat. When mixture comes to a full boil, adjust the heat and simmer until vegetables are tender, 20 to 25 minutes. Discard the cinnamon stick. Stir in the spinach, chickpeas, lime zest and juice and cook until spinach is wilted and curry is heated through, 3 to 5 minutes more. Season with salt and pepper.

To assemble the dish: Divide the curry among 4 bowls and garnish each serving with chopped cilantro.

Serve your guest a cold one from Cape Cod Beer Company (page 86).

Brewster Fish House

In the 1950s the building that now houses Brewster Fish House was a farm stand and was then turned into a gladiola farm. "I kept the original sign (see photo, right)," says owner Vernon Smith. Vernon has had the place since 1982, when his brother and he ran it as a fish market. "We knew nothing about retail. It could have been a scene from the *I Love Lucy Show*, but my intentions were always to turn it into a restaurant," he says.

The food is American cuisine that uses as many kinds of local produce and products as possible. "Cape Abilities in Dennis is a big player for our products, as are Tim Friary's Cape Cod Organic Farm in Barnstable and Ron Becker in Brewster," says Vernon.

Vernon and Melissa have always created a nice atmosphere in the Fish House. The service is friendly and professional and the food is good quality and comes out promptly .

Chef Shareff Badewy started cooking when he was eight years old. "I used to watch my mother in the kitchen," Chef Badewy says. "My father was from Cairo and my mother from Staten Island, so the cuisine was an eclectic mix in our house." The menu runs the gamut from seafood dishes to steaks and vegetarian dishes.

The restaurant does not take reservations, so get there early if dining in the summer months.

2208 Main Street, Brewster, MA 02631, (508) 896-7867, brewsterfish.com

BREWSTER OYSTER TARTARE WITH HUCKLEBACK CAVIAR, PRESERVED LEMON, HEIRLOOM TOMATO, LUCKY SORREL

(Serves 4)

Recipe developed by Chef Jeremiah

1 preserved lemon
2 Brandywine tomatoes
1 red onion
1 bunch scallions
1 bunch chives
2 lemons (not preserved)
12 Brewster oysters
6 tablespoons extra-virgin olive oil
Sea salt
Freshly ground white pepper
1 ounce huckleback caviar or other good grade of caviar
Crushed ice (buy crushed ice or chop ice cubes in a food processor)
Rockweed for garnish
4 white napkins
12 sprigs lucky sorrel

Dice the preserved lemon, tomatoes, and red onion. Slice the whites of the scallion on a bias. Chop the chives very fine. Cut the other 2 lemons (not preserved) into segments and dice. Combine all these in a mixing bowl.

Shuck the oysters, slice width-wise, and set aside, making sure to save the oyster liquid. Clean the shells and set aside. In a small bowl, combine the oysters with the tomato/lemon mixture and the olive oil. Season the mixture with sea salt and fresh ground white pepper.

To assemble the dish: Place the napkins on plates, then a layer of the ice and seaweed. Put 3 oyster shells on each plate and fill the shells with the oyster mixture. Top each with caviar and a sprig or two of lucky sorrel.

The Brewster Store
Groceries & General
Merchandise

The Brewster Store building was built as a two-story church
by the Universalist Society in 1852 at a cost of $5000. This
was the society's second building, the first having been across
from the old town hall. However, a steady decline in the
congregation during the ensuing decade which included the
Civil War, led to the decision to sell the church building and

its property located at Carlton E. Sears Square in the heart of Brewster. Now the building is home to the Brewster Store.

This is one of the oldest country stores on Cape Cod with a unique history. Here you can find everything from oil lamps and parts, clothing, food, candy, books, toys and other unique items like advertising, antiques, and a collection of World War II posters. There is also an antique wooden cranberry separator, and a waterline metal ship diorama of Kiel Harbor in 1938.

It is a great place to visit and have a scoop of old fashion ice cream in the ice cream parlor at the back of the store.

1935 Main Street, Brewster, MA 02631, 508-896-3744, info@brewsterstore.com

Cafe Edwige

When you walk down Commercial Street in Provincetown, keep an eye out for the flight of stairs that leads to the most popular breakfast place in town. It's on the bay side, opposite the old library, and right near Freeman Street. This flight of stairs leads you to a narrow covered porch, perfect for breakfast, dinner, or just a cocktail. Step into the building and you're in an airy loft–like dining room where you can enjoy everything Cafe Edwige has to offer.

Opened in 1974, Edwige was the place to go for breakfast for many years. Then, in 1999, owner Nancyann Meads decided to offer her chef the opportunity to create a dinner menu. Now you'll find day trippers, vacationers, and locals here morning and night. The staff is friendly, unpretentious, and talented. Every year they create the most amazing floats and costumes for the annual Carnival parade in August. And, of course, the food is divine.

Nancyann was born and raised in Provincetown, as were her mother and father, and the restaurant is named in honor of her mother. Her father was a boat builder and finish carpenter. Nancyann is a charming, elegant lady who has created a family-like atmosphere in the restaurant. She says, "Growing up in Provincetown was wonderful! I started working here as a waitress in 1974 and did that for seventeen years. Then I decided to buy the place. Now I have been in business thirty-seven years."

Cafe Edwige is known for its signature drinks as well as tasty omelets and Lobster Benedict. The restaurant has a strong following, so try and get there early for breakfast or make reservations for dinner.

333 Commercial Street, Provincetown, MA 02657, (508) 487-4020, edwigeatnight.com

LOBSTER BENEDICT

(Serves 2)

FOR THE DIJON BEURRE BLANC:

1 cup dry white wine, such as
 sauvignon blanc
¼ cup sliced shallots
2 tablespoons champagne
 vinegar
1 tablespoon Dijon mustard
Zest from 1 lemon, plus 2
 tablespoons juice
2 sprigs fresh thyme
1 bay leaf
¼ cup heavy cream
1 cup (8 ounces) cold unsalted
 butter, cut in cubes
Pinch sea salt
2 slices Portuguese bread, or
 any other freshly baked bread
¼ cup unsalted butter
2 tablespoons fresh lemon juice
 (from 1 lemon)
1½ cups fresh cooked lobster
 meat, cut in bite-size pieces
2 poached eggs
1 tablespoon minced fresh
 chives

For the Dijon beurre blanc: Combine the white wine, shallots, vinegar, mustard, lemon zest, thyme, and bay leaf in a small, nonreactive saucepan over high heat. Bring to a boil, then reduce heat to low and simmer until reduced to ¼ cup. Raise the heat to medium and add the cream, simmering until reduced by half; the liquid should be thick enough to coat the back of a spoon. Begin adding the cubed butter, one piece at a time, whisking constantly. Add each piece just before the last piece has completely melted, until all the butter is incorporated. Remove from heat and whisk in the lemon juice and salt. Strain the sauce into a clean saucepan and keep warm until serving time.

To assemble the dish: Grill or toast the bread and divide between two serving plates. Heat the butter and lemon juice in a sauté pan and add the lobster meat, stirring to heat through. Spoon the lobster over the toasted bread. Top with the poached eggs and a spoonful of Dijon beurre blanc. Garnish with chives and serve with home fries or field greens.

Try one of the Cafe's signature drinks for your brunch.

The Cape Sea Grille

The Cape Sea Grille is in an 1852 old sea captain's house and located on Sea Street just off of Route 28 in the heart of Harwich Port.

The husband-and-wife team of Douglas and Jennifer Ramler purchased The Cape Sea Grille in 2002, and Doug has been praised for his excellent fresh local seafood dishes. "I buy 99 percent local," says Chef Ramler. "I have fishermen in the area from whom I buy all my fish, and I use farmers like Veronica Worthington of Tuckernuck Farm in West Dennis, Tim Friary of Cape Cod Organic Farm Inc. in Barnstable, and Cape Abilities in Dennis for my produce. My philosophy is consistency and flavor first!"

Jennifer runs the front of the house in between caring for their two young children. The Cape Sea Grille has a cozy, comfortable atmosphere, and the service is friendly and professional.

The tables are far enough apart and not crowded. If you get a table in the back of the restaurant, you will have a little view of blue water. It is a perfect place to dine on a summer's night, then stroll down one block to the beach for a larger view of Nantucket Sound. Like most restaurants on Cape Cod, The Cape Sea Grille has a seasonal liquor license and is only open from April to New Year's Eve.

31 Sea Street, Harwich Port, MA 02646, (508) 432-4745, capeseagrille.com

OVEN-ROASTED COD WITH AUTUMN VEGETABLES
(Serves 4)

FOR THE ROOT VEGETABLES:
2–3 tablespoons extra-virgin
    olive oil
1 pound celery root, peeled and
    cut into ¾ x ½-inch rectangles
1 pound purple-top turnips,
    peeled and cut into ½-inch
    cubes

FOR THE CELERY CONFIT:
2–3 tablespoons extra-virgin
    olive oil
3 celery stalks, bias-sliced to
    ¼-inch thickness

FOR THE COD:
2–3 tablespoons extra-virgin
    olive oil
4 (7-ounce) skinless cod fillets
Salt and pepper to taste

For the root vegetables: Heat 1 tablespoon oil in a large sauté pan over medium-high heat. Add the celery root and cook, stirring and turning often, until tender and golden brown, about 10 to 12 minutes. Transfer to a plate to cool.

Add another tablespoon of oil to the pan and cook the turnips the same way as the celery root. Transfer to a plate to cool. Vegetables can be prepared one day ahead; cover and refrigerate until serving time.

For the celery confit: Heat the oil in a medium-size saucepan over medium-low heat and add the celery. Cook, stirring and turning, until the celery has lost its crunch but is not mushy or browned, about 12 to 14 minutes. Transfer to a plate to cool. Celery can be prepared a day ahead; cover and refrigerate until serving time.

For the cod: Preheat oven to 425°F. In a very large ovenproof sauté pan, heat the oil over high heat until it just begins to smoke. Season the cod with salt and pepper and lay fillets in the pan without touching. Cook until undersides are browned and move easily in the pan, about 2 to 3 minutes; turn and brown the second side. Place the pan in the oven and roast until the cod is just cooked through, 6–8 minutes.

For the stir-fry: While the cod is in the oven, drain the endive in a colander, tossing to remove excess water. Heat oil in a large sauté pan over medium-high heat. Add the Napa and cook, stirring constantly until wilted, 2 minutes. Add the shiitakes to the pan and continue cooking and stirring until mushrooms soften, about 3 to 4 minutes more. Repeat with the endive, and then add the celery confit, garlic, thyme, parsley, and salt and pepper; heat through.

For the pomegranate beurre blanc: When the fish is ready, place a piece on each dinner plate and cover loosely to keep warm. Return the hot pan to the stove over high heat. Add the wine, scraping the pan to loosen any browned bits, and reduce by half. Turn the heat to low and whisk in the butter, one piece at a time, until sauce is emulsified. Whisk in the cream, lemon juice, and salt and pepper to taste. Add the pomegranate molasses to taste; you may not need it all.

To assemble the dish: Place the root vegetables on a baking sheet and reheat in the oven alongside the cod. When hot, portion the vegetables with the fish. Divide the stir-fry among the plates and drizzle the beurre blanc over all.

FOR THE STIR-FRY:
1 head Belgian white endive, sliced lengthwise to ¼-inch thickness and submerged in lemon water to prevent browning
2 tablespoons extra-virgin olive oil
½ pound Napa cabbage, cored and shredded
½ pound shiitake mushroom caps, sliced to ⅛-inch thickness
1 clove chopped garlic
½ teaspoon chopped fresh thyme leaves
2 tablespoons chopped fresh parsley
Salt and pepper to taste

FOR THE POMEGRANATE BEURRE BLANC:
½ cup white wine
½ cup cold unsalted butter, diced
1 tablespoon heavy cream
1 teaspoon fresh lemon juice
Salt and pepper to taste
1 tablespoon (about) pomegranate molasses

Ceraldi's

Chef Michael Ceraldi offers a seven-course nightly menu based on the day's freshest local ingredients. "We opted to offer a prix-fixe nightly menu to our customers," says Ceraldi, "so we could honor the moment, the day's catch, and locally harvested ingredients—so our customers could taste Cape Cod. We feel passionate that food is best when you can taste where it has come from." Ceraldi aspires to tell a story through food that pays homage to what he values— love, family, food, friendship, and nature. "We are enjoying the best of what is available, while making sure our future generations can do the same. I rely upon sourced ingredients that help protect our ecosystem by encouraging sustainable and Earth-courteous harvesting techniques and building lasting relationships with local farmers, fisherman, hunters, gatherers, and beekeepers."

Ceraldi's is open from May to October. During the winter months, Chef Ceraldi teaches cooking classes and caters elegant dinner parties all over the Cape and Boston area.

15 Kendrick Avenue, Wellfleet, MA 20667, (508) 237-9811, Ceraldicapecod.com

CHILLED MUSKMELON (CANTALOUPE) SOUP
(Serves 4)

Serve the soup with smoked chili oil drops on top and crispy Prosciutto di Parma slices on the side.

FOR THE SMOKED CHILI OIL:
3 cups olive oil
2 heaping tablespoons smoked
    paprika
1 heaping tablespoon ground
    chili pepper

FOR THE CRISPY PROSCIUTTO
    DI PARMA:
Have the deli slice ¼ pound
    prosciutto (or speck if
    available) as thin as possible.

FOR THE SOUP:
1 ripe chilled muskmelon
    (cantaloupe), about 6 inches
    in diameter
Juice of one lemon
1 cup whole-milk plain Greek-
    style yogurt
1 tablespoon local honey
Salt to taste

To make the smoked chili oil: Mix all ingredients in a heavy-bottomed sauce pot. Allow mixture to simmer on low for 5 minutes. Remove from heat and let sit for one hour. Carefully pour off oil leaving the chili residue at the bottom of the pot. (A coffee filter can also be used.) Pour into an airtight bottle.

To make the crispy Prosciutto di Parma: Arrange the prosciutto slices to lie flat on a piece of parchment on a cookie sheet. Bake in a preheated oven at 375°F until crisp, about 5-8 minutes.

To make the soup: Peel and seed the melon then cut into about one-inch chunks. Purée melon in blender; once smooth add remaining ingredients and purée until combined. Garnish with fresh mint and crispy prosciutto.

Chatham Bars Inn

As you travel down the Cape, you find many treasures with a long history like the Chatham Bars Inn. In 1707 an affluent landowner, Squire Richard Sears, raised cattle and sheep on this property. Having twenty-five acres of waterfront property, he divided the land and in 1912 a Boston stockbroker, Charles Handy, acquired the land with the concept of building a hunting lodge for Boston vacationers. He built the inn with nine cottages that still stand today.

The inn has always been known for its food, especially seafood and New England fare. For the last six years, Chef Anthony Cole has taken over the kitchen and created new and innovative dishes using as much local produce and ingredients as possible. He told me about his new concept for the main dining room, Stars Steakhouse: "A cart of Midwestern grain-fed and dry-aged beef is rolled to your table, you pick your choice cut of steak, and then it is brought to the kitchen and cooked to your liking." There are also a variety of homemade sauces to choose from, like a red wine reduction and truffle foie gras, plus several gourmet sides like sautéed wild mushrooms, haricot verts, roasted fingerling potatoes, and caramelized garlic. Accompanying the entree are fresh organic vegetables grown in their newly purchased farm on 6A in Brewster.

Chef Cole went on to tell me about the extraordinary place they have for creating and enjoying a dessert after a meal: "We converted what used to be the chef's kitchen into a dessert lounge. It has comfortable cushions, couches, chairs, and tables. So when you finish dinner, you go to the lounge and can watch the chef preparing the desserts. There is a video camera and a wide overhead flat screen TV. We have a dessert called 'the Risk.' It is the chef's creation and changes all the time."

Besides Stars Steakhouse, there are three other restaurants at the inn: The Sacred Cod Tavern (open year-round); and the Veranda House, which serves lighter fare; and the Beach House Grill. The Varanda House and the Beach House Grill are only open in the summer months. They also cater special events and have pit-style clambakes that are a big hit during the summer.

297 Shore Road, Chatham, MA 02633, (508) 593-4978, chathambarsinn.com

CEDAR PLANKED SALMON

(Serves 4)

FOR THE VINAIGRETTE:

2½ cups red wine vinegar
½ cup sugar
¼ cup red onion, peeled and
    sliced thin
½ shallot, peeled and sliced thin
2 tablespoons honey
1½ tablespoons Dijon mustard
3 garlic cloves, peeled and sliced
2–3 teaspoons kosher salt
½ teaspoon chopped fresh thyme
¼ vanilla bean, split and seeds
    scraped
Pinch ground black pepper
⅔ cup vegetable or canola oil

FOR THE POTATOES:

½ pound fingerling potatoes,
    washed and dried
3 tablespoons olive oil
Salt and pepper to taste
2 tablespoons unsalted butter

FOR THE MUSHROOMS:

½ pound assorted wild
    mushrooms, cleaned,
    trimmed, and cut up if large
3 tablespoons olive oil
Salt and pepper to taste

FOR THE SALMON:

2 cedar planks, soaked in water
    for 2–6 hours
4 (6-ounce) salmon fillets
4 teaspoons oil for coating fillets
Salt and pepper to taste

For the vinaigrette: Put all the vinaigrette ingredients except the oil in a saucepan and simmer over medium heat until reduced by half. Transfer the hot mixture to a blender and, holding a folded towel firmly against the lid, puree until smooth. With the blender running, pour oil very slowly through the hole in the lid to create an emulsion. Set aside and keep warm.

For the potatoes: While the vinaigrette is reducing, preheat oven to 350°F. Toss potatoes with olive oil and season with salt and pepper. Spread the potatoes on a baking sheet and bake until tender, 20 to 30 minutes. Halve the potatoes lengthwise. Melt the butter in a large sauté pan over medium-high heat, add the potatoes, and cook, stirring occasionally, until golden brown. Season with additional salt and pepper to taste; keep warm.

For the mushrooms: Increase the oven temperature to 450°F. Toss the mushrooms with olive oil and season with salt and pepper. Spread the mushrooms on a baking sheet and bake until tender and slightly caramelized, 12 to 15 minutes. Remove from oven and keep warm.

For the salmon: Preheat a gas or charcoal grill to about 350°F (medium hot). Lightly coat salmon fillets with 1 teaspoon oil per fillet, season with salt and pepper, and place on the grill grate fleshy round side down. Cook just until dark grill marks form and fish loosens easily from the grill, about 3 to 5 minutes. Using a flat metal spatula, carefully rotate the fillets one-quarter turn, and continue to cook until more dark grill marks form, creating a crosshatched pattern on the fish. Transfer the salmon to the cedar planks, grilled side up. (Fish should not be cooked through.) Place the cedar planks on the grill with a little space on all sides for heat and airflow. Cover the grill and cook until fish is just opaque all the way through, 10 to 12 minutes. Transfer the fish fillets to four dinner plates.

To assemble the dish: Divide the hot buttered potatoes among the plates. Toss the warm mushrooms, frisée, and diced tomatoes with ⅓ cup warm dressing and season with salt and pepper. Arrange some salad beside each salmon fillet and drizzle everything with a little more dressing.

TO ASSEMBLE THE DISH:
2 heads frisée lettuce, leaves separated, washed, dried, and trimmed
¼ cup seeded, diced plum tomatoes
Salt and pepper to taste

The Cook Shop

The Cook Shop was opened in 1976 in what was once an old house on historic Old King's Highway. It is located next to the Lemon Tree Pottery Shop and is still owned and operated by

the same family. The Cook Shop has two floors of kitchen items and gourmet foods, gadgets, gourmet cookware, and everything you will ever need in your kitchen.

The sister shop, in another building, is The Tabletop Shop. Here you will find another two floors dedicated to tableware, linens, and everything to make a beautiful table setting.

One can spend a whole day in Lemon Tree Villages. You can even have lunch at Café Alfonso, next to The Cook Shop. It is a casual place to grab a sandwich and an espresso, and sit outdoors during the warm summer months.

1091 Route 6A, Brewster, MA 02631, (508) 896-7698, Cookshopcapecod.com

Clambakes

Like many areas along the New England coast, Cape Cod claims to be the birthplace of the clambake, but the Cape's claim is said to be the strongest, because we are the first part of North America that the Pilgrims set foot on. There is a lot of folklore centered on the

fact that the clambake originated with the Native Americans. The Native Americans probably did steam and cook some of their food on heated rocks covered with seaweed long before the *Mayflower* set sail. However, if this is true, it was not the clambake as we know it today. In the book *Clambake* by Kathy Neustadt, there is a quote by Jim Baker, a historian with the Plimoth Plantation (March 22, 1988), that says, "No one knows much about the history of the clambake. There have been a lot of assumptions made, but we've never had to prove them."

Today the clambake is a big social event for native New Englanders and vacationers. It ranks up there with other all-American eating institutions, such as the backyard barbecue, the Saturday night church supper, and the family picnic.

During the summer months the pit-style clambake is the most popular, especially along the seacoast. Curiously, the celebrated clam (steamers or little necks) is not the star in this culinary extravaganza; it shares top billing with the North Atlantic lobster. The supporting cast usually includes potatoes, onions, corn on the cob (but still in the husk), chorizo, hot dogs, and sausage. Sometimes chicken and sweet potatoes are added. The vegetables, clams, and meats are wrapped in cheesecloth and bagged separately for easy handling.

An authentic clambake starts early in the morning with the gathering of quantities of firewood and rocks the size of grapefruits. The wood is stacked and the rocks placed on top of the wood. The fire is lit, and the rocks are heated for several hours.

While the rocks are heating, a pit is dug. When the rocks are piping hot, about 450°F, they are tossed into the pit with a pitchfork. To generate steam, seaweed is heaped onto the rocks.

The food is then layered on the seaweed, sometimes in wood or wire frames. Food taking the longest cooking time goes on the fire first. The usual layering is potatoes, onions, lobsters, steamers, and corn. You can add chorizo, hot dogs, or sausage as the final layer if you like. It takes several hours for everything to cook.

Clambakes do not have to be large. Sometimes they can be prepared in barrels or new ash cans buried halfway into the ground to help seal in the heat. Rocks are heated and placed in the bottom of the barrel. Six inches of seaweed is added, then the food in layers. As mentioned above, food taking the longest cooking time goes at the bottom nearest the heat source. Seaweed is added between each layer.

MINI CLAMBAKE

Here is my version of a mini clambake that serves 4, using beer instead of water for steaming. It can be done in your own home, in your backyard, or on a stretch of beach over a campfire. You'll need a large kettle with a rack that will allow the food to sit 3 inches from the bottom of the pan. You can also use large stones from the beach. A good kettle to use is one meant for preserving and canning.

4 small onions

4 small red bliss potatoes

1–1½ quarts beer

4 (1½-pound) lobsters

4 ears corn in their husks

Steamers or littlenecks, about 1 dozen or more per person

8 hot dogs, 2 per person

1 pound butter, melted, divided into 4 small bowls

Lots of cold beer to drink

Put the rack in the pan upside down. Put the onions and potatoes on the rack. Add 1 quart beer, cover, and bring to a boil; steam 5 to 7 minutes. Uncover, check to see how much beer has evaporated, and add ½ quart more if necessary. Be sure there is always at least 1 inch of beer in the bottom of the pan!

Add the lobsters, corn, and steamers or littlenecks. They may be layered over the lobster and corn or put into a cheesecloth bag. Finally, lay the hot dogs on top. Cover and start timing the cooking from the moment the steam escapes from under the cover. It should take 20 to 25 minutes for the food to cook.

Author's Note: If you are doing this at home, prepare your table while the food is steaming. I like to eat this outdoors. I cover my table with newspapers and have individual plates, nutcrackers, and small bowls for the butter. There is no elegant way to eat this meal. Put on your old shirt and dig in. Dunk everything in the butter including the hot dog!

LOBSTER STOCK

When everyone has had their fill of lobster, save the shells and make a stock. It can be used in a variety of ways like lobster bisque—or add a little to your next seafood dish or chowder.

Left-over lobster shells

1 bottle dry white wine

Water

Onion, celery, carrot, optional

Place all the shells in a large pot and crush them with a heavy object. Add a bottle of dry white wine and enough water to cover the shells. You may add a cut up onion, celery, and a carrot but it is not necessary. Bring to a boil, turn heat to low and simmer for about 45 minutes. Let cool, then strain into small containers and freeze until ready to use.

Places for Summer Clambakes
(Pit–Style and Steamed)

Chatham Bars Inn

297 Shore Road
Chatham, MA 02633
(508) 593-4978
chathambarsinn.com

The inn (see page 154) has pit-style clambakes from Memorial Day to Labor Day. They are family-friendly events that start at six o'clock every evening, Monday through Friday. There are games for the children and live entertainment. The evening ends with toasting s'mores by the fire pit.

Clambakes, Etc. . .

2952 Falmouth Road (Route 28)
Osterville, MA 02655
Jason Maguire, Sales
(508) 420-0500
clambakesetc.net

If you are in the Upper Cape and decide you want a pit-style clambake, contact Jason. He will help you with the planning for a minimum of fifty people.

Backside Bakes

Nick Moto and Michael Silvester, Owners
E-mail: nutonic@aol.com
(508) 527-9538
Facebook: backside bakes
Twitter: @BakesideBakes

Nick and Michael do family-style, customized clambakes for as few as seven and as many as sixty people. They can do a complete party, including everything from a raw bar to desserts.

The Lobster Trap Fish Market and Restaurant

290 Shore Road
Bourne, MA 02532
(508) 759-7600
lobstertrap.net

The Lobster Trap (see page 54) has been catering events for twenty years—everything from weddings and rehearsal dinners to company events and birthday parties—and clambakes are their specialty. They cover Cape Cod as well as Southeastern Massachusetts.

Eat Cake 4 Breakfast Bakery

Danielle is an artist when it comes to baking. The philosophy for her bakery and life is, "Food should be fun and delicious. People all over the world celebrate life with food, and pastries are the party favorite! I believe in high quality even for the most basic products and hope that my passion and love for food translates to our customers."

In Brewster, situated right off the Rail Bike Path you will find the Eat Cake 4 Breakfast Bakery. Danielle's elegant French bakery brings Paris to the Cape. She creates delectable breakfast treats, cakes, cookies, breads, and quiches. Grab one after a bike ride and savor its deliciousness. It is worth a special trip to the bakery to purchase one of her specialties.

If you want to impress guests at your next dinner party, I would suggest pre-ordering her fabulous Opera Cake: layers of dark chocolate and coffee butter cream between layers of almond sponge cake. Cut the cake into 1¼ x 4 inch slices with a touch of gold leaf on the corner of each slice. This elaborate cake serves eight. Total indulgence!

302 Underpass Road, Brewster, MA 02631, (508) 896-4444,
Eatcake4breakfastbakery.com

Hangar B Eatery

This is one of the fun places on Cape Cod for breakfast. It is open every day from 7 am–2 pm during the summer months, with limited hours in fall and winter.

The menu is creative and quite extensive––everything from eggs benedict to huevos rancheros. I had the delicious Lemon Ricotta pancakes. It is amazing what Chef Brian creates in his small kitchen. Along with his daily menu specials, he has a whole sideline of specialty items, like donuts, muffins, jams, and jellies. "When I started the baking-potato buttermilk doughnuts and muffins, the reaction was something I hadn't quite expected––people loved them! Now these items are sold independently downstairs so that people can come and pick those things up to go."

Hanger B is also available for catering private events either at the eatery or off-site.

240 George Ryder Road (Chatham Airport), Chatham, MA 02633, (508) 593-3655, hangarbcapecod.com

LEMON RICOTTA PANCAKES

(Makes about 12 to 14 pancakes)

1 cup all-purpose flour
1 teaspoon baking powder
1 teaspoon baking soda
½ teaspoon salt
¼ cup sugar
1 cup ricotta cheese, drained
½ cup buttermilk
3 eggs, separated
1 teaspoon vanilla
½ cup butter, melted and cooled
    plus more for greasing griddle
2 tablespoons lemon zest

Preheat the griddle to 375°F.

Whisk together flour, baking powder, baking soda, salt, and sugar in a small bowl. In a larger bowl, mix the ricotta, buttermilk, egg yolks, vanilla, ¼ cup of the melted butter, and lemon zest. Mix gently until well combined.

With a rubber spatula, stir the dry ingredients, a large spoonful at a time, into the ricotta mixture.

Beat the egg whites with a hand-held mixer in another bowl until firm light peaks form.

Stir 2-3 tablespoons of the egg whites into the batter to lighten it. Gently fold remaining egg whites into the batter.

Brush the grill with the remaining butter and pour ¼ cup of batter onto the hot griddle for each pancake. Cook evenly until bubbles form around edges, 1-2 minutes. Flip and cook evenly on other side, 1-2 minutes more. Repeat with remaining batter, buttering the griddle as necessary.

Hot Chocolate Sparrow

In 1989 Marjorie and Bill Sparrow took out a loan and opened their first "simple candy store," as they put it, in North Eastham. Marjorie's love for chocolate started in her home kitchen, where she made all the chocolate sold in the store.

In 1991 a summer shop, the Chocolate Sparrow, opened in Wellfleet Center. "Two years later Bill built this building from a hole in the ground, and we opened Hot Chocolate Sparrow. It is a café version of the one in Wellfleet. We try to make candy, food, and drink for the masses," Marjorie says.

The day I was there, Kathy Dufresne was making the toffee. "I have been making the candy for twenty-two years, and before that I was Marjorie and Bill's babysitter," she says. She was trained by Marjorie and now trains other candy makers here.

I watched Kathy make the toffee. "It is most important to use a candy thermometer," she says. "You can do it by eye, but I do not want to take the chance." She adds the nuts at about 270°F. She says, "I stir the mixture until it reaches 300°F, and then someone will come in and pour it for me."

Marjorie is proud of the shop she has created. It is now going on twenty-three years. "We are a great gathering spot for people in Orleans and the surrounding area," she says. "Because we are in the center of Orleans, it has become a meeting place for people of all ages, young and old. It is a place for people to come, hang out, and even work. During the summer months we hire a variety of different people; diversity is our motto, and my husband says we are like the United Nations. We have shared and taught a lot of people about coffee shops. We are the most popular place around."

Hot Chocolate Sparrow is the best candy café on the Cape, with lots of advantages like homemade special chocolates made on the premises, other candy, and good food and drinks. It is near the bike path and a great place to stop for a special treat. They are open at six thirty in the morning and close at eleven at night. They are closed just one day a year: Christmas Day.

5 Old Colony Way, Orleans, MA 02653, (508) 240-2230, hotchocolatesparrow.com

ENGLISH TOFFEE
(Fills 1 [12 x 17-inch] pan)

2 pounds butter
¼ cup water
4 cups superfine sugar
1 teaspoon liquid lecithin
2 cups chopped nuts, divided
2 cups milk chocolate, melted

Coat a rimmed, parchment-lined baking sheet with butter or nonstick cooking spray.

Melt the butter in a large, heavy-bottomed pot over medium heat. Add the water, then the sugar, stirring until sugar dissolves completely. Stir in the lecithin. Attach a candy thermometer to the side of the pan and raise the heat to medium high. Wash sugar crystals from the sides of the pan with a pastry brush dipped in water. Cook the syrup to 280°F, swirling the pan occasionally but not stirring the contents. Add 1 cup chopped nuts and continue cooking, washing down the sugar crystals again. When mixture reaches 296°F, quickly pour it onto the parchment-lined pan. When the candy is set, spread the melted chocolate over the surface and cover with the remaining nuts. When chocolate is firm, cut the toffee into squares.

Karoo South African Cuisine

Tucked in the back of a large building, off Route 6A, you will find Senette Groenewald's Karoo, the unique South African restaurant. Senette, originally from South Africa, started this small restaurant in Provincetown; now she has a much larger place with seating in a colorful dining room with unique décor. The menu is extensive, creative, and traditional South African food. There is also a patio for dining, and gardens surround the building during the warm weather.

Senette's unique homemade authentic sauces, chutneys, and spices used in her delicious cooking and grilling can be purchased in the restaurant, online, or by phone.

3 Main Street, Unit 32B, Eastham, MA 02642, (508) 255-8288, Karoorestaurant.com

KAROO'S CAPE MALAY STEW WITH SHRIMP
(Serves 1)

This is a delicious curry-based dish with assorted seasonal vegetables, perfect for anytime of the year.

FOR THE SHRIMP:
4 to 6 medium shrimp
1 tablespoon Karoo stew base
  (or make your own as shown
  below)
¼ cup coconut milk
½ to 1 cup mixed vegetables of
  your choice

FOR THE STEW BASE:
¼ teaspoon curry powder
Pinch of ground ginger
Pinch of garlic powder
Splash of soy sauce
¼ teaspoon peanut butter

To make the stew base: In a small bowl, mix together the ingredients into a paste.

To make the shrimp: Add stew base to a warm sauté pan. Add coconut milk and slowly heat and stir to dissolve paste. Add shrimp and vegetables and bring to a boil while stirring. Cook on a slow simmer until sauce reduces and thickens. Serve over rice with banana and fruit chutney.

Lola's Local Food Lab

Kim Shkapich (pronounced SKAH-PITCH) is an inventive lady. She was an important figure in the architecture and design field before she moved to Cape Cod in 2004 and opened Lola's Local Food Lab. She now makes and sells her tasty shrubs. They are made with local seasonal fruits, vegetables, and herbs—many from her own garden or from farms around the area. Some flavors include garden beet, cranberry apple, blueberry basil, Rose Farm rhubarb (named from the Truro farm that grows the fruit), black cherry, pear ginger, and cucumber dill. The list goes on, as she constantly comes up with new flavors.

The early English version of the shrub arose from the medicinal cordials of the 15th century, some of them containing vinegar. Kim's vinegary mixtures are infused with fruit juice, herbs, spices, and are sometimes used in mixed drinks. It all started with her mother making shrubs for her as a child.

I had several samples when I was in her shop which looks part chemistry lab and part kitchen. Her shrubs last for up to nine months and need to be refrigerated after opening. She is totally certified and makes her products under strict rules for safety.

Along with her delicious shrubs, Lola's Food Lab makes special small batches of hand-blended rubs, with some ingredients from her own garden. #1 Universal Magic Dust, spicy and hot, is perfect for flavoring meats, nuts, and even popcorn. Other favorites include #1A Magic Maple and #4 Bonfire Bright. All of Lola's products may be purchased online.

Addictive Culinary Alchemy, PO Box 3068, Wellfleet, MA 02667, (508) 349-1700, lolaslocalfoodlab.com

LOLA'S BLUEBERRY BASIL MOCKTAIL

2 ounces Blueberry Basil Shrub
8 ounces sparkling water
½ ounce fresh lime juice

Mix liquids and serve over ice in a Collins-style glass. Garnish with a cucumber spear.

STRAWBERRY RASPBERRY SPLASH

2 ounces Uncle Val's Botanical
    Gin
1 ounces Strawberry Raspberry
    Shrub
½ ounce framboise

Shake and strain into martini glass, or serve on ice and top with seltzer. Garnish with a fresh strawberry and a sprig of mint

LOLA'S BLUEBERRY BLOSSOM COCKTAIL

2 ounces Blueberry Basil Shrub
2 ounces vodka
2 ounces Pavan (a French
    liqueur of Muscat grapes and
    orange blossoms)

Pour ingredients over ice in a cocktail shaker and shake until frosty. Rim a martini glass with orange peel (optionally dip the peel in superfine sugar if you have a sweet tooth). Strain into the glass, and garnish with an orange slice or a sprig of fresh basil.

Mac's

During the summer months, the lines are out the door to get in. All three Mac's locations are lively places to have a good seafood dinner. The menu is Contemporary American, seafood, and sushi. Owner Mac Hay grew up on the Cape. He has built an empire and prides himself on serving the best fresh seafood around. Eating at any of his places, you will see why it is true.

Mac's Fish House, 85 Shank Painter Road, Provincetown, MA 02657, (508) 487-6227, Open All Year, For catering, market, fish shop, and shipping, contact (800) 214-0477, info@macseafood.com

Mac's Seafood on the Pier, 265 Commercial Street, Wellfleet, MA 02667, (508) 349-9611, Open April to October

Mac's Shack, 91 Commercial Street, Wellfleet, MA 02667, (508) 349-6333, Open April to October

MAC'S CRACKER-CRUSTED BLUEFISH

(Serves 3)

"This recipe comes from our grandmother and is still our family's favorite way to eat bluefish. It is delicious and very simple to make, but one important note: do not add any salt! The crackers and bacon drippings provide all you need. We like to crumble the bacon over a salad and serve it alongside the fish."

1 pound fresh bluefish fillet, cut
    into 3 portions
3 slices bacon
1 large egg
½ cup finely crushed Ritz
    crackers

Take the bluefish out of the refrigerator and bring to room temperature (this will help the fish cook evenly). Preheat the oven to 350°F.

Cook the bacon in an iron skillet over medium-high heat until crisp. Transfer to a plate and serve it crumbled on top of a side salad, if desired. Reserve the bacon fat in the pan.

Whisk the egg in a medium size bowl for the egg wash. In another bowl, add the crushed crackers. Dip both sides of the fish in the egg wash and then in the cracker crumbs. Heat the skillet containing the bacon fat; when the fat is hot, not smoking, sear the fish 1-2 minutes per side, and place the pan with the fish in the oven. Bake for 5-6 minutes until done. Remove the pan from the oven and remove the fish to paper towels for a few minutes before serving.

Optional: Serve fish on a bed of cream spinach and whipped potato on the side.

Napi's Restaurant

"You are in a restaurant that was never a restaurant!" says Napi Van Dereck, owner of Napi's Restaurant. The restaurant was originally home to the antiques business that Napi and his wife, Helen, ran. "Whatever possessed us to open a kind of 'lobster in the rough' restaurant I will never know," he says. That was in 1974.

Since he couldn't get a bank to lend him the money he needed to build a restaurant, Napi decided to build their restaurant himself. Luckily, he was a carpenter and builder. With the help of other townspeople and a salvage yard in Quincy, his dream started to take shape. The "lobster in the rough" concept went by the wayside. "I'd lived in the Middle East and played the mandolin," he says. "We got a band together, played in the restaurant, and turned the concept into a Middle Eastern theme restaurant. Because we literally did not owe any money except to pay off the plumbers and people like that, we opened the restaurant and were able to survive. And actually made a profit that year."

The decor was determined by the antiques shop Napi and Helen had started, as well as by some old wood found at that salvage yard in Quincy. In addition, Napi and Helen felt the restaurant should represent the town and its many artists. Once you're seated, look around and see the brick mural done by Conrad Malicoat, the sculptures by Al Davis, and the paintings by local artists from Napi's own collection.

The menu has become more varied over the years and is now quite eclectic. The chef is Everard Anthony Cleary, known to everyone as "Tony." He serves up entrees and appetizers that hail from the Middle East, Brazil, and Jamaica. "I started here in April 1999. I'm originally from Kingston, Jamaica. I went back to Jamaica and brought my family here," says Tony. "Napi's is like a family to me."

That family feeling resonates with tourist and locals. The restaurant is open for dinner year-round, and does a nice lunch in the off-season. Stop by and feast your eyes and your palate.

7 Freeman Street, Provincetown, MA 02657, (508) 487-1145, napis-restaurant.com

KING'S FEAST
(Serves 2)

FOR THE TOMATO SAUCE:

2 tablespoons olive oil

1 onion, peeled and diced

1 large garlic clove, chopped

1½ cups fish stock or bottled clam juice

1 cup whole peeled canned tomatoes with juice

4–5 fresh basil leaves

Splash white vermouth

FOR THE SEAFOOD:

1 (1¼-pound) live lobster

1 (8-ounce) fresh cod fillet, skinned

14 mussels, rinsed well and beards removed

4 littleneck clams, shells scrubbed of sand

4 sea scallops, cleaned and membranes removed

4 medium whole shrimp

½ lemon, for squeezing

2 fresh basil leaves, sliced

2 tablespoons chopped fresh parsley

For the tomato sauce: Heat the oil in a very large sauté pan over medium heat. Add the onion and garlic and cook, stirring constantly to avoid burning the garlic, until onion is softened and translucent, about 8 minutes. Add the fish stock or clam juice, tomatoes, basil, and vermouth. Adjust heat so mixture simmers gently for 10 minutes.

For the seafood: Meanwhile, bring a large pot of salted water to a boil for the lobster. When the water reaches a rolling boil, add the lobster head first and cook 9 to 10 minutes. Transfer to a shallow bowl and set aside. When the sauce is ready, nestle the cod, mussels, clams, scallops, and shrimp in the bubbling sauce and continue to cook until the shells open and the fish is opaque all the way through, about 5 minutes.

To assemble the dish: Transfer the contents of the sauté pan to a large, shallow serving bowl. Cut the lobster in half, if desired, and position on top of the feast. Squeeze lemon juice over everything and garnish with basil and parsley. Serve immediately.

Orleans Wine and Spirits

When I was in Umbria a year ago, leading a culinary tour, I had the privilege of visiting the Antonelli Organic winemakers in Montefalco. There we had lunch and sampled their wines. I brought several back to the villa to serve with our dinner in my cooking class.

After returning to the Cape, I called Robert Valchuis, owner of Orleans Wine and Spirits, and found he imports wines from the same vineyard. Two of them, the white Grechetto and the red Baiocco from Umbria are now our standard table wines.

If you are looking for fine Italian wines on Cape Cod, this is the place!

9 West Road, Orleans, MA 02653, (508) 255-2812, (800) 240-1811, Orleanswine.com

RISOTTO WITH SAGRANTINO WINE AND RADICCHIO

(Serves 6 to 8)

Sagrantino di Montefalco is an Italian wine made with 100% Sagrantino grapes in the Province of Perugia in Umbria. It is one of Antonelli's high-end delicious wines. I developed this recipe around the wine.

6 cups chicken broth (you many not use all of it)
2 tablespoons extra-virgin olive oil
1 tablespoon butter
2 shallots, minced
1 cup prosciutto (about 1-ounce slab), diced
1 cup Italian rice
1½ cups Sagrantino wine
1 head of radicchio (should make 2 cups)
½ cup finely grated fresh Parmigiano Reggiano
2 tablespoons butter
Salt and pepper to taste

Gently heat the broth and keep warm over low heat.

Heat the olive oil and butter in a saucepan over medium heat. When hot, stir in the shallots. Cook 1-2 minutes. Add the prosciutto, cook for another 2 minutes, and add the rice, stirring to coat with the oil and butter. After about 2 minutes, when rice has taken on a pale, golden color, stir in 1 cup of the radicchio, and cook for 1 minute, then pour in wine, stirring constantly until the wine is fully absorbed. Add ½ cup broth to the rice, and stir until broth is absorbed. Continue adding broth ½ cup at a time. In the last addition of broth, stir in the remaining cup of radicchio and continue stirring until the liquid is absorbed and the rice is al dente.

The risotto will take about 18-20 minutes total to cook. Remove it from the heat and add the Parmigiano Reggiano and butter and mix well. Season with salt and pepper.

Food From the Sea

While fishing as an industry has changed on Cape Cod, there are still fishermen who go to sea and supply many Cape restaurants and markets with the catch of the day.

Cape Cod Commercial Hook Fishermen's Association

ccchfa.org

The Cape Cod Commercial Hook Fishermen's Association is a nonprofit group started in 1991 by the local fishing fleet, who were determined to conserve marine resources through sustainable fishing. It has become the leading community fisheries organization in the region. In the travel edition of *Saveur* magazine, the association was commended for its work. The rules and regulations surrounding fishing on Cape Cod have greatly changed the industry and are hot-button topics down here. A visit to their website provides a great deal of information. The association also provides a variety of events such as the annual Hookers Ball, a fundraiser for the local fishing community.

Barnstable Sea Farms

Les Hemmila
barnstableseafarms.net

It was one of those beautiful September fall days on Cape Cod.
I had arranged with Les Hemmila of Barnstable Sea Farms
to photograph him in the waters of Barnstable Harbor where
his oyster farm is located. Les told me he got his grant in 1991
and then started his business. He also
told me a few interesting facts about
oyster farming. "In the cultivation of
oysters, the oysters have to be moved
around at least once a month by
stacking the racks and shifting them
around. This prevents the oysters
from getting a distorted shape. The
oysters' shape has to be perfect in
order to sell to raw bars. We want to
make the most presentable product
out there." Barnstable Sea Farms is a
big proponent of the "Buy Fresh Buy
Local" movement on Cape Cod, and
their delicious oysters are featured by
name at many local restaurants.

The Naked Oyster

Florence and David Lowell
nakedoyster.com

The Naked Oyster is a restaurant in Hyannis (see page 124).
It's included in this section because it has its own oyster farm.
Executive Chef Florence Lowell truly believes in quality, and

when she learned she could farm her
own oysters she went for it. "The town
keeps all of the grants," she says.
"When someone gives up or doesn't
maintain his or her grant, then it is
assigned to the next person on the
list. You have to pay for the grant and
abide by the rules of the town, and the
grant must be properly maintained,
environmentally. In Barnstable one
can have up to about two acres. The
grant must be renewed each year.
And you must tell the town how many
oysters you have harvested and pay a
small fee."

Barnstable Oyster

Kevin Flaherty and Tamar Haspel
barnstableoyster.com

Kevin Flaherty was a
commodities trader
and Tamar Haspel was
an author. They were
living in New York
when they decided to
make a big change. In
2008 they moved full-
time to Cape Cod. Both
can do their work out

of their home, but they also wondered what else they could
do out here on the Cape. Kevin became friends with Florence
Lowell of the Naked Oyster. In January 2009 bad weather was
on the way and Florence asked Kevin for some help with her
oyster grant. Kevin pitched in and from then on he, along with
Tamar, was hooked. He also met Les Hemmila of Barnstable
Sea Farms around this time. Les was a real inspiration, and
today Kevin and Tamar have their own farm and a distributor
in Brooklyn. Their oysters can be found in many upscale New
York restaurants.

PB Boulangerie Bistro

PB Boulangerie owner and chef Philippe Rispoli, a native of Lyon, France, is bringing the taste of French country cooking to Cape Cod. Philippe decided to open his restaurant in South Wellfleet because he had vacationed there for many years. The building, once a small clam shack, has been turned into a delightful bakery and bistro. The aroma hits you as you walk through the door—that is, when you finally do walk through the door, because there is usually a line snaking down the walkway. Once you're in, you find a wall of beautiful fresh-baked breads and glass cases filled with delicious French pastries. The beamed ceiling in the bakery adds to the ambience. Past the bakery is a sixty-seat restaurant where the walls are covered with antique copper molds and pans. The bar is inlaid with shells and faces the open kitchen where Chef Rispoli works his magic. At the far end of the bar is a Limonaire, a hand-cranked instrument made of wood that produces music you would hear in the streets of Paris. Chef Rispoli says, "I brought it to Wellfleet to give my customers a taste of France."

On the day I was there, Chef Rispoli was preparing three beautiful country pâtés. He worked like an artist and, in his charming French accent, explained to me what he was doing. "I make everything from scratch, with quality ingredients. I lay the foie gras on top of the forcemeat and cook the pâtés very slowly." He then pulled the pastry crust over the long loaves of ingredients. On the counter he created a long braid to be placed down the center of each crust.

PB Boulangerie Bistro is well worth the trip down the Cape for that unique French experience.

15 Lecount Hollow Road, South Wellfleet, MA 02663, (508) 349-1600, pbboulangeriebistro.com

BRAISED SHORT RIBS

(Serves 8)

FOR THE WINE REDUCTION:
3 bottles (750 ml) dry red wine

For the wine reduction: Place the red wine in a large saucepan over medium heat. When the wine is hot, quickly and carefully wave a long lit match just above the surface to light it. When the flames die down, raise the heat to bring the wine to a boil. Continue cooking until wine is reduced by half. Remove from heat and set aside.

For the short ribs: Preheat oven to 350°F. Combine the flours, salt, crushed pepper, dried thyme, garlic powder, and cloves in a bowl; toss with the ribs to coat.

Heat the oil in a very large (8- to 10-quart) Dutch oven or ovenproof saucepan over medium-high heat. Sear the ribs until they are well browned, about 5 minutes per side, working in batches if necessary (crowding the pan will inhibit browning). As they are done, transfer the ribs to a plate and set aside.

Discard all but 1 tablespoon of fat from the pot and add the shallots, carrots, celery, leek, garlic, parsley, bay leaves, and thyme sprigs. Sauté over medium heat until the vegetables are browned, being careful not to burn the bottom of the pan, about 8 minutes. Add the tomato paste, cook 1 minute, and remove from heat. Let mixture cool slightly, then transfer to a food processor and blend until smooth.

Return the pan to high heat and add about 1 cup veal or beef stock to deglaze the pan, scraping up all the browned bits stuck to the bottom. Add the rest of the stock, the wine reduction, vegetable puree, and seared ribs with their juices and bring to a boil.

Cover the pot and place in the oven to braise until the ribs are fork tender, about 3 hours. Bring to room temperature and then chill the ribs in the liquid overnight.

To assemble the dish: Remove the pot from the refrigerator and scrape off the surface fat. Place the pot over medium-high heat and bring to a simmer to thoroughly reheat. Transfer the ribs to a platter and boil the pan juices until reduced by half. Strain the sauce through a fine sieve into a clean pot, discarding the solids. Season with salt and pepper and return the ribs to the sauce. Reheat gently to serve.

FOR THE SHORT RIBS:

2 tablespoons wheat flour

2 tablespoons malted barley flour

2 tablespoons salt

2 tablespoons black peppercorns, crushed with a mallet or the side of a heavy knife

1 tablespoon dried thyme

1 tablespoon garlic powder

¼ teaspoon ground cloves

8 beef short ribs (about 5 pounds), trimmed of excess fat

2 tablespoons vegetable oil

8 large shallots, peeled and separated and large lobes halved

2 medium carrots, peeled and diced

2 celery stalks, trimmed and cut into 1-inch pieces

1 medium leek, washed well and coarsely chopped and dark green leaves discarded

8 large garlic cloves

6 sprigs Italian flat-leaf parsley

2 bay leaves

2 sprigs fresh thyme

2 tablespoons tomato paste

3 quarts veal or beef stock

Salt and pepper to taste

Pisces

Sue Connors and Ann Feeley have created a charming restaurant with a cozy five-seat bar in the seaside town of Chatham. Wainscoting on the wall is topped with original artworks by local artists, and tables covered with white linen have parchment paper menus resting on them. With dishes like Pan-Roasted Chatham Littleneck Clams and Lobster Ravioli, it's clear that they have taken the restaurant's motto, "All good things come from the coast," to heart.

Sue and Ann opened their restaurant in 2001. "We started working together twenty-seven years ago in big hotels and then in smaller restaurants. Then we started looking for a place of our own," says Sue. "I was working in Chatham for a few summers when this place became available. Everyone said don't do it! But we did it!" They both come from conservative blue-collar families. "My family's philosophy is you do not give up a job with security, a weekly paycheck, and a job with benefits. My brother saved his bonus for when we went belly up." Luckily Sue's brother can keep that bonus, because Pisces has been a smashing success.

2653 Main Street (Route 28), Chatham, MA 02659, (508) 432-4600, piscesofchatham.com

CHATHAM LITTLENECK CLAMS IN PORTUGUESE KALE STEW

(Serves 4 as an appetizer or 2 as a main course)

FOR THE STEW:

2 tablespoons canola or olive oil
⅓ cup diced onions
1 teaspoon chopped garlic
Pinch crushed red pepper flakes
1 bay leaf
¾ cup sliced Portuguese chorizo
¾ cup peeled, diced carrots
¾ cup diced red potatoes,
    skin on
1 (24-ounce) bottle clam juice or
    lobster stock (page 136)
1 bunch kale, washed, dried,
    stemmed, and leaves
    coarsely chopped
½ cup canned cannellini beans,
    rinsed and drained
⅓ cup diced fresh tomatoes
32 littleneck clams, shells
    scrubbed in cold water to
    remove sand
Focaccia or other rustic Italian
    bread, sliced thick
Softened Garlic Butter (page 13)
    or olive oil

For the stew: Heat the oil in an 8-quart, straight-sided sauté pan over medium-high heat. Add the onions and cook, stirring, just until onions are translucent, about 5 minutes. Add the garlic, red pepper flakes, and bay leaf; cook 1 minute more. Add the chorizo and cook until it begins to release some of its oil, then add the carrots and potatoes and continue cooking until vegetables begin to soften. Add the clam juice or lobster stock, raise the heat to high, and bring to a boil. Stir in the kale, beans, and tomatoes and when mixture returns to a boil, lower the heat so the stew simmers until the kale turns dark green and is very tender, 5 to 8 minutes.

Arrange the clams in a single layer over the stew and cover tightly with a lid or foil. Let the clams steam until they open, 5 to 10 minutes. (Discard any clams that do not open.) Taste the broth and adjust seasoning, adding a little more water if it's too salty.

To assemble the dish: Use tongs to divide the clams among warm shallow pasta bowls and ladle the stew over them. Serve with bread for dipping, brushed with garlic butter or oil and toasted or grilled if desired.

The Farmers Who Feed Us

Many of the local farms offer what is known as a Community Supported Agriculture (CSA) program. You pay a fee to the farmer at the beginning of the season, then pick up a box of freshly harvested produce on a weekly basis.

Not Enough Acres Farm

Owners: Jeff and Beth Deck
107 Sesusit Road
East Dennis, MA 02641
(508) 737-3446

Not Enough Acres Farm sells hats, gloves, and bags, as well as vegetables, fruits, herbs, and honey. Jeff and Beth Deck own Shetland Islamic sheep, and Beth spins and makes all the items from their wool. When the Decks started the farm, they didn't have enough property to get a tax break on their farm, so they leased the property across the street in order to get the necessary 5.25 acres. That's how the farm got its name. The Decks have now been on the property for thirty-three years.

Cape Abilities Farm

458 Main Street (Route 6A)
Dennis, MA 02638
(508) 385-2538
capeabilities.org

There are two Cape Abilities Farm locations: one in Dennis, which operates a farm stand and the greenhouses, and another in Marston Mills, which is a working farm. All produce grown in Marston Mills is transported to Dennis to be sold. The farms provide paid employment for people with disabilities who work in all areas of farm management. The farm sells to many of the restaurants on Cape Cod, including FIN, the Brewster Fish House, the Chatham Bars Inn, the Naked Oyster, and Pain D'Avignon. Cape Abilities also has a number of business partnerships. The Centerville Pie Company is one such partner and now has most of its pie production done in the Hyannis branch, where over forty disabled adults are employed. Other partners are the Woods Hole Oceanographic Institute and Cape Cod Beach Buckets. Most recently Cape Abilities has been providing space for Cape Cod Saltworks to harvest salt.

Cape Cod Organic Farm

Owner: Tim Friary
3675 Main Street (Route 6A)
Barnstable, MA 02630
(508) 362-3573
capecodorganicfarm.org

The farm is certified organic and specializes in fruits (starting with delicious strawberries in early summer), cut flowers, herbs, and vegetables into the early winter. Tim also raises Heritage Breed Pigs for pork and has laying chickens for eggs.

Tuckernuck Farm

Owner: Veronica Worthington
89 Fisk Street
West Dennis, MA 02670
(508) 364-5821

Tuckernuck Farm was founded in 1998 on an acre of land. Veronica Worthington sells her variety of heirloom lettuce, which she is noted for, at farmers' markets and her farm stand, which is open from the end of May to November. She also sells wool and wool roving from her heritage sheep. The farm also offers the CSA program.

Buy Fresh Buy Local

The theme "Buy Fresh Buy Local" is the slogan at all farmer's markets on Cape Cod. The season starts in May and continues into November.

Early spring farmers bring out many kinds of produce (or plants) they have started in green houses like lettuces, peas, tomatoes and many of the plants we use for our gardens, both vegetable and flower. For me, I prepare my gardens beforehand and find it easier to buy pre-started plants rather than seeds I have started myself. I go to the markets, pick my plants, and have an instant garden by Memorial Day.

As the season progresses so does the abundance of fruits and vegetables in the markets. And don't forget lobsters, seafood, artisanal cookies, breads, jams and jellies.

When fall approaches, I look forward to the many varieties of apples, pumpkins, and squashes. Each year I find a new variety of something I have not seen before.

The Red Inn

The Red Inn is located at Provincetown's far west end. This charming establishment dates back to 1805 and has a long history of dignitaries and celebrities who have stayed here. President Theodore Roosevelt and Mrs. Roosevelt stayed at the inn when they came for the laying of the cornerstone for the Provincetown Monument in 1907. Over the years people like Joseph Kennedy and the Nixons had special rooms here. Gloria Swanson was a visitor here. She had her favorite artist, Ada Rayner, paint the mural over the fireplace in the room across from the bar. In fact a small dining room at the inn is named for Ada Rayner, who was part of the Provincetown art colony and married to Henry Hensche, founder of the Provincetown School of Art.

"It was a landmark in the fifties and sixties and fell on hard times in the mid-eighties and throughout the nineties," says David Silva, one of the owners. "The three of us bought it in 2001 and renovated and opened it in 2002. We brought it to where it is today. Over the years we have been very fortunate to have lots of publicity and lots more celebrities come and stay. Norman Mailer's movie was filmed here."

Silva is a third generation Provincetown native. "My family owned the Dairy Queen for forty-five years, my grandfather ran the bank, my uncle was principal of the high school, and I am very fortunate to own such a historical landmark in the town where I grew up."

For starters, try the lobster sliders served on two mini buns or the seafood sampler with oysters, clams, shrimp, and lobster tails. The main courses run the gamut from fresh local seafood to steaks, chops, chicken, and duck. One of the Red Inn's signature dishes is the lamb chops.

The view from the bar and dining room is one of the best on Cape Cod. Whether you're having a drink or dining, the ever-changing Provincetown Harbor, the lighthouse at Long Point, and the sandy cliffs along the shores of the Outer Cape are sights you will long remember.

15 Commercial Street, Provincetown, MA 02657, (508) 487-7334, theredinn.com

HERB-MARINATED LAMB CHOPS

(Serves 4)

FOR THE MARINADE:

½ cup honey

¼ cup Dijon mustard

2 tablespoons minced fresh
rosemary

1 tablespoon minced fresh thyme

1 tablespoon minced fresh basil

½ teaspoon salt

¼ teaspoon coarsely ground
black pepper

12 baby lamb chops

For the marinade: Combine the honey, mustard, herbs, and salt and pepper in a medium bowl and mix well.

Place the lamb chops in a shallow dish large enough to hold them in a single layer. Spread the marinade over the lamb, turning to coat all sides. Let stand at room temperature for 30 minutes, or cover and refrigerate overnight.

Grill or broil the chops to desired doneness, about 4 to 5 minutes per side for medium-rare. Transfer to a plate, cover loosely with foil, and allow to rest 5 minutes before serving.

Snowy Owl Coffee Roasters

Snowy Owl Coffee Roasters is set back off Route 6A in the same building as Great Cape Herbs. Manuel Ainzuain is originally from Peru. He came to the Cape from San Francisco with his wife Shayna Ferullo, who used to summer here, and infant daughter. All together, they opened Snowy Owl.

When you walk into this barn-like interior, heated in the winter with a wood stove, the fragrant aroma of freshly brewed and roasting coffee permeates the room. Snowy Owl Coffee House has become a central gathering place for the community. When I was there people were working on laptops, a few children were quietly playing in the corner, while other people were sitting around enjoying the customized individual cups of filter drip coffee or a cappuccino.

For people who love a great cup of coffee, this is the place for lattes, iced coffees, espressos with a decorative top, and flavored coffee drinks. It is all here in this rustic, warm, and friendly café.

2624 Main Street, Brewster, MA 02631, (774) 323-0605, Socoffee.com

ESPRESSO GELATINA CAFFÈ (ESPRESSO COFFEE JELLY)

(Serves 4)

This jelly may also be made with left over strong coffee. It is perfect served with a little heavy cream over the top or a dollop of whipped cream. Add a biscotti or your favorite cookie on the side.

1 package, unflavored gelatin
4 tablespoon sugar
3 tablespoons cold water
2 cups fresh brewed espresso

In a small saucepan, combine gelatin, sugar, and cold water. Add 1 cup of the coffee and boil over high heat. Stir until the gelatin and sugar have dissolved. Pour the mixture into a small bowl with remaining coffee, cover with plastic wrap, and chill in the refrigerator until solidified about 6 hours.

Sunbird Food Truck and Sunbird Kitchen

One day last summer while driving down the Cape, I noticed a beautifully painted food truck in Wellfleet. I had to stop and investigate. This was my introduction to the Sunbird Food Truck, with its beautifully lettered motto, "Eat well . . . on the Fly," painted over the serving window, and to owners J'aime and Christian Sparrow. Christian is from Cape Cod, and J'amie is from Connecticut. They have known each other since childhood. J'aime's passion is food and Christian's is design. They spent ten years in San Francisco, where J'aime worked in the restaurant business and Christian was in interactive design and advertising. They moved to Cape Cod in 2010 and bought the truck. J'aime became the chef, and Christian was fortunate enough to bring several of his clients with him. He also hand painted the truck.

"We both have a passion for nostalgia and the salty side of Cape Cod," Christian says. "And, of course, the good, simple food that we serve in the Sunbird." J'aime has created a delicious, interesting menu, much of it using local ingredients. The menu is displayed on a blackboard propped against the truck. The day I was there, the featured items were a Fish Taco on a Corn Tortilla, a Gourmet Hot Dog (this is usually on the menu), and a Market Sandwich with fresh mozzarella and oven-roasted tomatoes. Most days you can also grab a breakfast sandwich with local eggs to order and smoked bacon. Pull in and order something "on the fly" or stay and eat at one of the nearby picnic tables.

2520 Route 6A, Wellfleet, MA 02667, (508) 237-0354, birdinthesun.com

SUNBIRD BRUSSELS SPROUTS

(Serves 4–6)

FOR THE BRUSSELS SPROUTS:

1 pound brussels sprouts, trimmed, halved, and quartered if large

Salt for boiling water

FOR THE PECANS:

2 cups pecans

2 tablespoons brown sugar

2½ teaspoons olive oil

2 teaspoons Chinese five-spice powder

1½ teaspoons salt

½ teaspoon crushed red pepper flakes

FOR THE CITRUS BUTTER:

½ cup unsalted butter, room temperature

1 tablespoon finely chopped shallot

Zest of 1 orange

1 teaspoon honey

¾ teaspoon ground cinnamon

½ teaspoon salt

FOR THE PANCETTA:

1 teaspoon olive oil

⅛ pound pancetta, thinly sliced

1 tablespoon olive oil

¼ cup cider vinegar

For the brussels sprouts: Blanch the sprouts in boiling, salted water just until al dente, 4 to 5 minutes. Transfer to a bowl of ice water to stop the cooking. Drain very well and set aside. This can be done a day ahead; cover and refrigerate until ready to serve.

For the pecans: Preheat oven to 375°F. Toss the nuts, brown sugar, olive oil, five-spice powder, salt, and red pepper flakes in a bowl until evenly coated. Spread in a single layer on a baking sheet lined with parchment paper and bake until golden and fragrant, 7 to 9 minutes. Let cool on a baking sheet, then roughly chop and set aside. This can be done ahead; store in an airtight container at room temperature until ready to serve.

For the citrus butter: Place the butter, shallot, orange zest, honey, cinnamon, and salt in a mixing bowl. Mash and stir with a fork until creamy and incorporated. Set aside. This can be done a day ahead; cover and refrigerate until ready to serve.

For the pancetta: Heat the oil in a sauté pan just large enough to hold the pancetta slices. When the oil is hot, add the pancetta and cook until crisp. Drain on paper towels and crumble. Set aside.

Heat olive oil in a very large sauté pan or seasoned cast iron skillet. Add the blanched brussels sprouts and cook, tossing occasionally, until browned, 3 to 7 minutes. Reduce heat to low and add a generous spoonful of citrus butter. Toss again until butter is melted and sprouts are well coated. Increase heat to medium-high and add the vinegar, tossing to distribute. Cook to reduce the vinegar, about 1 minute more, and remove from heat. Add about ¾ cup chopped seasoned pecans and garnish with the crumbled pancetta.

The Talkative Pig

Chef Jeff Mitchell and his wife Terri are proud to serve Mediterranean-inspired dishes made from fresh local ingredients and traditional family recipes. Jeff had been in the food service industry most of his life. Then in 2015 Jeff and Terri decided to open their own place.

When I was there, Terri was running around making her homemade biscotti for the restaurant. In passing, she told me jokingly, "This is our retirement!"

They make their own pizza dough, delicious desserts, and all entrées, mostly Italian-inspired. The food on the menu is crafted carefully at the restaurant. "We want people to enjoy the food as much as we enjoy preparing it," said Chef Mitchell.

2642 Main Street, South Chatham, MA 02659, (508) 430-5211, thetalkativepig.com

GRANDMA NANCY'S HALF CHICKEN

(Serves 1)

This is a recipe handed down to Jeff from his grandmother.

1 half chicken, bone-in
2 tablespoons olive oil
1 large onion sliced
1 teaspoon fresh thyme leaves
1 teaspoon fresh minced garlic,
   about 1–2 cloves
1 (15-ounce) can diced tomatoes
1 cup chicken broth
½ cup dry white wine
1 teaspoon fresh thyme leaves
Salt and pepper

Heat the olive oil in a sauce pan and brown the chicken until golden brown. Remove from pan and keep warm.

Add the onion and thyme to the same pan, adding more oil if necessary, and sauté until onions are translucent and start to brown. Add the garlic during the last 2 minutes.

Add the chicken broth and white wine, deglazing the pan, and reduce to half. Add the tomatoes with their juice, reduce heat to medium, and simmer for about 30 minutes. Add salt and pepper to taste. Put the chicken back in the sauce, cover the chicken, and cook for another 25 minutes.

Truro Vineyards

The story goes like this: Dave Roberts went out for a bike ride one day while vacationing in Truro and came home with a vineyard. Dave had just retired after a career in the wine and spirits industry, and operating a vineyard had always been a dream of his. "Cathy and I are from Connecticut and have been coming here since our honeymoon forty-seven years ago," says Dave. "This vineyard has been in operation since 1991, and we've owned it for six years. It's working! We have a good business plan, and we are making it work! Our whole family—our son and two daughters—are equal owners and share the tasks of the operation."

It is worth a trip here just to look at the beautiful setting of Truro Vineyards. The house and lands have been in existence for two centuries. Passed down through the Hughes and Rich families, the property inspired two paintings by Edward Hopper. Located just off Route 6, it's a great place to stop for a tour and a wine tasting. The vineyard has a wonderful pavilion out back that can host special events of up to sixty-five people. My favorite is the barrel room, where the wine is stored. The barrels line one wall, and the air is filled with the smell of fermenting grapes. On each side of the huge sliding wood doors that lead to the fermenting rooms are murals painted by Dave and Cathy's nephew, Mark Melnick. One is a map of Cape Cod and the other is of the whole family working in the vineyards. While used frequently for rehearsal dinners, I think the barrel room would be a great place to throw a party for any occasion!

The Roberts family has all bases covered at Truro Vineyards. There's the wine, the wine and gift store, tours, places for events, the sweeping view of the vineyards, and the beautifully manicured estate. This is a unique and different place on Cape Cod.

11 Shore Road, North Truro, MA 02652, (508) 487-6200, trurovineyardsofcapecod.com

DAVE'S CHEESEBURGERS

(Serves 4)

2 pounds ground beef (85% lean and 15% fat)
1 teaspoon olive oil
1 teaspoon Worcestershire sauce
Pinch sea salt
Pinch steak seasoning (Canadian mix works well)
½ teaspoon garlic flakes
4 slices American cheese or your favorite cheese
4 hamburger buns

Place the ground beef in a large bowl along with the olive oil, Worcestershire sauce, salt, steak seasoning, and garlic flakes. Mix gently by hand to combine, taking care not to compress the ingredients. Shape the meat into four thick patties. Start grilling on a hot grill to sear both sides, then cook to medium-rare on medium heat, adding cheese and covering 2 minutes before done. Serve burgers on warm buns with Dave's Famous Onion/ Blue Cheese topping.

DAVE'S FAMOUS ONION/BLUE CHEESE TOPPING

¼ stick (2 tablespoons) butter
2 tablespoons olive oil
1–3 onions, depending on size
4 cloves garlic, chopped
¼ cup red wine (Truro Vineyards Cabernet Franc), or your favorite Cabernet Franc
Pinch Italian mixed seasonings
¼ pound blue cheese

Heat a cast iron skillet on medium-high heat. Add butter and olive oil. Add onions and garlic and sauté until onions have browned, being careful not to burn the garlic. Add wine and Italian seasonings and deglaze the pan, about 2 to 3 minutes, until wine is reduced to a rich thick sauce. Stir in the cheese until melted. Cover to keep warm until burgers are ready.

Twenty-Eight Atlantic at the Wequassett Resort and Golf Club

If you're visiting the Cape and looking for an elegant dining experience, this special restaurant at the Wequassett Resort and Golf Club in Harwich is your place. The Wequassett Resort offers a bit of paradise, with twenty-seven acres of salt marshes and woodlands and breathtaking views of Pleasant Bay and the Atlantic Ocean. Executive Chef James Hackney, who hails from Leicestershire, England, says, "We want to offer a dining experience that parallels the luxury of Wequassett," and his food sure does that.

Chef Hackney began his culinary career by working in his parents' Garden Hotel, a quaint hotel in the English countryside, where farm-to-table was a way of life. And now, here on Cape Cod, he has cultivated relationships with local farmers, fishermen, and purveyors. Following his parents' example, he's using these local ingredients and putting his own creative twist on classic favorites. Try the Pleasant Bay oysters, Atlantic halibut, or the butter braised lobster to see how Chef Hackney re-creates these Cape Cod favorites. The presentation is elegant and formal, as is the beautiful, spacious dining room. The wait staff is attentive; everyone in the restaurant is there for you, making sure your experience is an exceptional one. Reservations are a must. Make sure to ask for a table by the window that faces the bay. If you time it right, you can add a spectacular sunset to what is sure to be an extraordinary meal.

2173 Route 28, Harwich, MA 02645, (508) 430-3000, wequassett.com

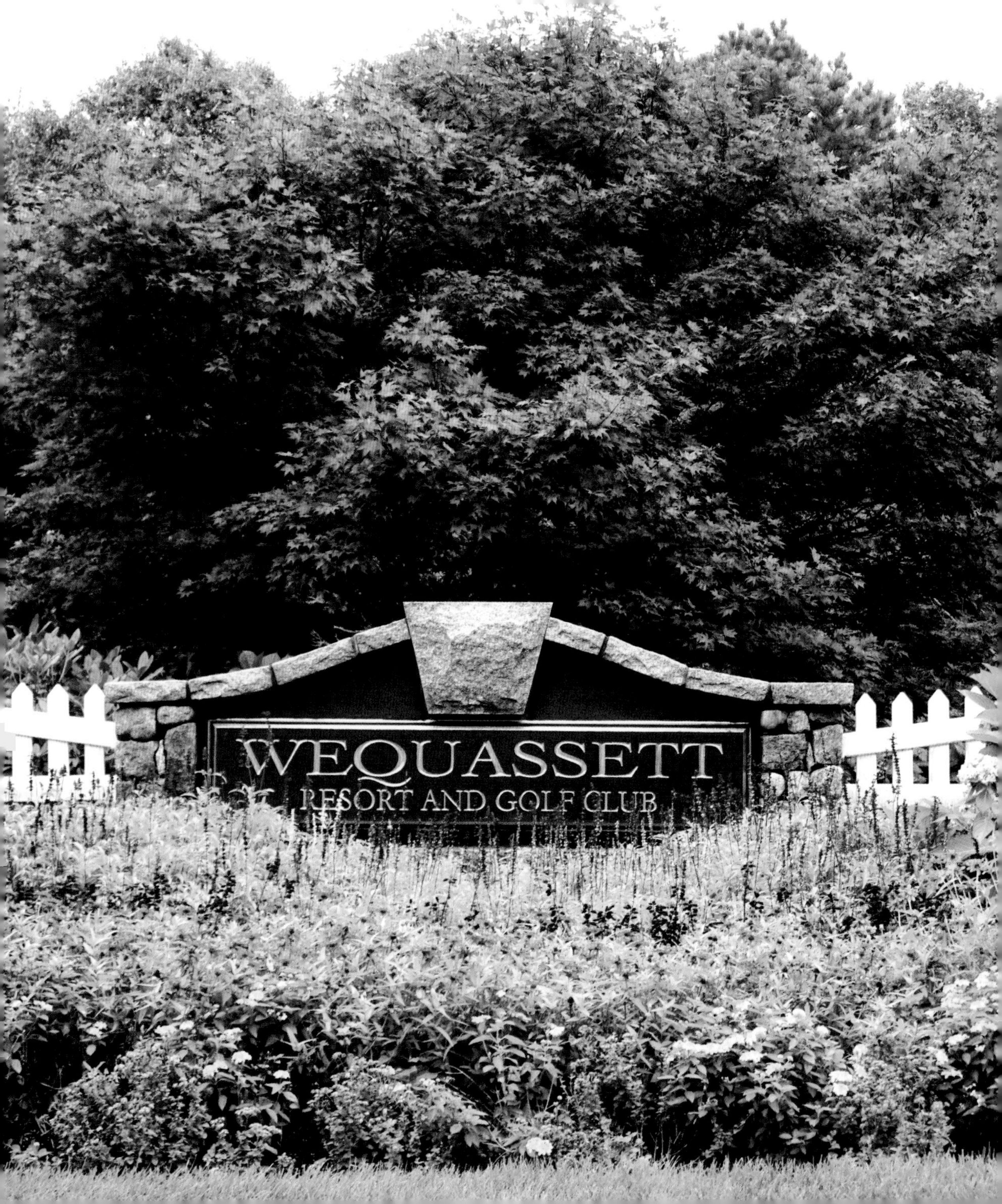
WEQUASSETT
RESORT AND GOLF CLUB

APPLE TARTE TATIN

(Serves 4)

FOR THE CRUST:
1 sheet puff pastry (half of a
   17-ounce package), thawed
   but kept cold

FOR THE TARTE:
4–5 Granny Smith apples,
   peeled, cored, cut in half and
   quartered
5 tablespoons sugar, divided
1 teaspoon cinnamon
3 tablespoons water
3 tablespoon butter

FOR THE HONEY CINNAMON
   SOUR CREAM:
¾ cup sour cream
6 tablespoons honey
⅓ cup confectioner's sugar
¼ teaspoon ground cinnamon

For the crust: Unfold the pastry sheet on a lightly floured work surface. Invert a 6-inch-round cake pan on top of the dough and cut around it to form a circle of pastry slightly larger than the pan. Transfer the dough circle to a baking sheet and refrigerate until needed. Reserve the rest of the dough for another use.

For the tarte: Combine the apples, 1 tablespoon sugar, and cinnamon in a large bowl; toss to coat. Set aside.

Preheat oven 375°F. Put the remaining sugar and water into the bottom of a 6-inch cake pan and place over medium-high heat until the sugar turns golden brown. For a darker caramel, continue to cook but be careful not to burn the syrup. Stir in the butter until melted; tilt the pan to caramelize the sides. Use potholders to remove pan from heat.

Carefully position the apples flat side down (point side up) in a circle in the pan. Place the cake pan on a baking sheet for easier handling; bake until apples are just tender when poked with a paring knife, about 15 to 20 minutes. Remove apples from oven.

Place the cold puff pastry circle directly on top of the apples, tucking the edges down around the apples, and return to the oven. Bake until pastry is puffed, golden, and looks dry, about 20 minutes. Transfer tarte to a wire rack to cool slightly, 5 to 10 minutes.

Make sure that none of the pastry is stuck to the edges of the pan and invert a rimmed serving platter on top of the cake pan. Using potholders and working over the sink, hold the cake pan and platter firmly together and flip them so that the platter is on the bottom and the cake pan is on top. Set the whole thing down on the counter and carefully lift off the cake pan (juices will be hot). Replace any apples that stick to the skillet.

For the honey cinnamon sour cream: Combine sour cream, honey, sugar, and cinnamon in a bowl and mix well. Cover and refrigerate until serving time.

To assemble the dish: Using a long, sharp knife, cut the tarte into desired pieces and place a slice on each dessert plate. Pour a spoonful of the cream over each piece and serve immediately, while the apples are slightly warm.

CARAMELIZED SCALLOPS
(Serves 4)

2 pounds sea scallops, about 4 to 5 per person

FOR THE PEA PUREE:
2 pounds freshly shelled English peas, or best-quality frozen peas
2 tablespoons chopped fresh mint
1 cup water
1 tablespoon extra-virgin olive oil

FOR THE CARROT GNOCCHI:
½ pound carrots, peeled, trimmed, and cut into 2-inch chunks
5 tablespoons freshly grated Parmigiana Reggiano cheese, divided
3 tablespoons all-purpose flour
1 egg yolk
Pinch freshly grated nutmeg
Sea salt and freshly ground black pepper to taste

12 slices (about 6 ounces) prosciutto
½ cup (4 ounces) unsalted butter
½ lemon for squeezing
Pea tendrils or mint sprigs for garnish

For the scallops: Rinse scallops in ice water and lay out on towels to air dry in refrigerator, 1 to 2 hours before searing. This will help with the searing process.

For the pea puree: Blanch fresh peas in boiling salted water for 3 minutes; drain well. Transfer peas to a blender and add the mint. With the blender running, slowly add the water to form a smooth puree; repeat with the olive oil. Transfer pea puree to an airtight container and refrigerate until ready to use. Rinse out the blender to use for the carrot gnocchi.

For the carrot gnocchi: Cook the carrots in boiling salted water until tender, about 10 to 12 minutes; drain well. Transfer carrots to the blender and puree until smooth. Add 3 tablespoons grated cheese, flour, egg yolk, nutmeg, sea salt and freshly ground black pepper to taste. Blend until evenly combined.

Scrape carrot dough into a piping bag fitted with a medium-size tip. Bring salted water to boil in a wide, shallow saucepan and have a bowl of ice water and a pair of clean kitchen scissors ready. Holding the piping bag over the saucepan, squeeze out the carrot dough and snip off 1-inch lengths so they drop into the boiling water. Boil until gnocchi rise to the surface, about 1 to 2 minutes, and use a slotted spoon to immediately transfer them to the ice bath; remove and pat dry. There should be about 20 gnocchi in all.

For the prosciutto: Preheat oven to 375°F. Line two rimmed baking sheets with parchment paper. Divide prosciutto slices between the baking sheets, laying them flat. Bake until fat turns golden and meat darkens, about 10 to 15 minutes.

To assemble the dish: Warm the pea puree in a small stainless steel saucepan over low heat, stirring often until heated through; set aside. Melt half the butter in a large sauté pan over high heat. Add the scallops and sear on both sides until caramelized on both sides, about 1 to 3 minutes per side. Transfer scallops to a plate. Wipe out the sauté pan and add the rest of the butter over high heat. Add the gnocchi and sauté, turning occasionally, until golden brown.

Dollop about 2 tablespoons warm pea puree in the middle of each of four dinner plates and use the back of a spoon to push the puree across the plate to create a design. Squeeze lemon juice over the scallops and gnocchi in the pan and then arrange them on top of the pea puree on each plate. Lean slices of crisp prosciutto against the scallops, trying not to cover the whole plate but giving it a nice design, then add pea tendrils or fresh mint as a garnish.

Viera

I first met Ben Porter when he was chef at the Belfry Inn & Bistro in Sandwich. Ben is a creative chef and has also worked at The Glass Onion in Falmouth. In 2014, Porter and his wife Angela opened their own place on the Dennis/Harwich line. The couple, turned what use to be Friendly's, into a smart modern American cuisine restaurant with inspired food. Angela greets you as you enter with a friendly welcome which extends from the wait staff as well. To the left is the bar and the smiling face of Josh, the bartender. If you are looking for lively conversation eating with other people, the bar is your place. For a quieter romantic night, there are a few hi-tops behind the bar and a 56 seat, understated dining room with booths beyond. Some with a view of the open kitchen. The menu, like the place, is familiar and comfortable.

11 Route 6A, West Harwich, MA 02671, (774) 408-7492, Vieracapecod.com

SAUTEED CAPE SEA SCALLOPS WITH CELERIAC PUREE, CITRUS VINAIGRETTE, FENNEL SCALLION COMPOTE

FOR THE CELERIAC PUREE:
2 tablespoons butter
2 tablespoons vegetable oil
1 small onion, diced
1 small leek, whites only, diced
2 pounds celeriac (celery root), peeled and diced
1 quart vegetable stock
1 cup heavy cream
1 ounce Sambuca
2 bay leaves
Salt and white pepper

FOR THE CITRUS VINAIGRETTE:
Juices of each lemon, lime, and orange, mixed together
1 tablespoon finely diced shallot
1 tablespoon honey
4-5 basil leaves, chopped
1 cup extra-virgin olive oil

FOR THE FENNEL SCALLION COMPOTE:
1 small head of fennel, diced fairly small
1 bunch scallions, chopped
4 tablespoons extra-virgin olive oil
2 ounces white wine
Zest of 1 lemon
Small pinch of cayenne pepper

To make the celeriac puree: Heat oil and butter in a large 6 quart sauce pot over medium heat. Add onions, leeks, and bay leaf, and sweat over medium heat for 5 minutes. Add Sambuca and cook for 2 minutes. Add vegetable stock and diced celeriac, raise heat to high and boil for 20 minutes or until celeriac is soft. Add heavy cream and bring back to a boil. Once cream begins to bubble remove from heat. Season with salt and white pepper to your liking. Transfer to food processor and puree in small batches. Chill for reheating or keep in a warm area for serving. The celeriac puree can be made a couple days in advance and reheated.

To make the vinaigrette: In a medium bowl, add citrus juices, honey, basil, shallot, salt, and white pepper to taste. Continuously whisk bowl and slowly drizzle in oil a little at a time. The vinaigrette can be made one day in advance and held in the refrigerator.

To make the fennel scallion compote: In a 2-quart sauce pan, add olive oil and diced fennel, and sweat over medium heat for 5 minutes, stirring frequently to avoid browning. Add chopped scallions and cook for 2 minutes. Add white wine and cook until mostly evaporated. Remove from heat and stir in lemon zest, cayenne pepper, salt, and the rest of the olive oil. Let cool to room temp and reserve for serving. The compote can be made 2 hours in advance and kept at room temperature.

To sauté the scallops: Heat a sauté pan large enough to hold the scallops without touching each other or work in small batches. Add 2 tablespoons vegetable oil and heat until just slightly smoking. Season scallops and carefully add to pan. Sauté until golden brown.

Once brown, turn off heat, flip scallops and add butter to pan. Once butter is melted coat the scallops with the butter, and remove from pan and drain on paper towel.

To assemble the dish: Arrange celeriac puree and scallops on plate and garnish with the compote and vinaigrette.

FOR THE SCALLOPS:
1½ to 2 pounds large sea scallops
2 tablespoons vegetable oil
2 tablespoons butter
Salt and white pepper to taste

the
wicked oyster

50 main street

The Wicked Oyster

There are many historical buildings on Cape Cod that have been turned into successful restaurants. The Wicked Oyster is one of them. Its original structure housing the dining room dates back to 1750. The building was floated across the bay from Billingsgate Island. The area is just south of Great Island at the mouth of Wellfleet Harbor at Jeremy Point and is visible only at low tide.

The restaurant with its old slanted wood floors is comfortable and evokes that familiar feeling of being in someone's home. The restaurant is open for breakfast, lunch, and dinner during the summer months.

50 Main Street, Wellfleet, MA 02667, (508) 349-3456, wickedo.com

Winslow's Tavern

Tracy and Phillip Hunt have been running Winslow's Tavern since 2005. Tracy manages the front of the house, while Phillip runs the kitchen.

Phillip had moved from Johannesburg, South Africa, to New York City to pursue a career in fine art. Tracy was working in New York as a film producer. Their paths crossed while working on a documentary film, and they got married shortly after. They had shared a dream of opening a tapas bar in the city, but when Tracy's family, who already had a restaurant, decided to open another one in Wellfleet, their dream changed course. "Tracy's parents told us about this tavern in the center of Wellfleet, and we jumped at it and here we are," says Phillip.

Phillip learned to cook from his mother, who owned several restaurants in Johannesburg. "I was a form of cheap labor and was dragged into the kitchen doing everything. I got to know fast what she expected of me in her kitchens," explains Phillip. Clearly those expectations were high. His use of local ingredients like Wellfleet oysters, Chatham cod, littleneck clams, monkfish, and mussels has made Winslow's Tavern one of the most popular restaurants on the Lower Cape.

The building that houses the restaurant has been a fixture in Wellfleet since 1805. Once a sea captain's house, it was also the home of Massachusetts governor Channing Cox in the 1920s. Rumor has it that during this time President Calvin Coolidge was a guest. The building has been a restaurant for over forty years. Upgraded by its present owners, the tavern has a warm, open feel. If you're here on a warm summer night, make sure to ask to dine on the patio with its wonderful grape arbor.

316 Main Street, Wellfleet, MA 02667, (508) 349-6450, winslowstavern.com

GRILLED LOCAL SWORDFISH

(Serves 4)

FOR THE PAN TOMATOES:

2 teaspoons extra-virgin olive oil
1 teaspoon minced shallots
1 teaspoon minced garlic
1 teaspoon crushed red pepper
  flakes
½ cup Nicoise olives, pitted and
  halved
¼ cup large capers, drained
1 cup white wine
4 vine ripe tomatoes, cut into
  ¾-inch cubes
1 teaspoon sugar
½ cup packed fresh parsley
  leaves
1 teaspoon grated fresh lemon
  zest
Salt and pepper to taste

FOR THE PAN SWORDFISH:

2 teaspoons olive oil
Salt and pepper to taste
4 (10-ounce) swordfish fillets

FOR THE ROMAINE HEARTS:

2 teaspoons extra-virgin olive oil
Salt and pepper to taste
2 romaine hearts, halved
  lengthwise

For the pan tomatoes: Heat the oil in a large sauté pan over low heat. Add the shallots, garlic, and red pepper flakes and cook slowly just until shallots are translucent but not brown, about 10 minutes. Add the olives and capers, stirring to coat. Raise the heat to high, and when it is sizzling hot, add the wine. Cook, stirring, until most of the wine has evaporated, about 6 to 8 minutes more. Add the tomatoes and sugar and toss until the tomatoes just start to collapse. Stir in the parsley leaves and lemon zest and season to taste with salt and pepper. Set aside.

For the swordfish: Oil and season the swordfish and place over a medium-hot fire until opaque all the way through, about 4 minutes per side.

For the romaine hearts: While the fish is cooking, heat the oil in a large sauté pan over medium heat. Season the romaine hearts with salt and pepper and arrange them cut sides down in the oil. Cook until golden brown on all sides, turning carefully with tongs to keep the leaves neatly together.

To assemble the dish: Gently reheat the tomatoes. Arrange the romaine hearts on four serving plates, one half for each serving, fanning out the leaves. Place a swordfish fillet on top of the romaine and divide the tomatoes over the fish. Lightly drizzle with a quality extra-virgin olive oil and serve immediately.

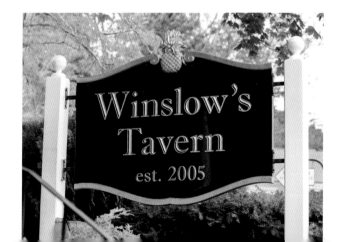

GRILLED SWORDFISH

(Serves 4 to 6)

FOR THE SWEET CHILI SAUCE:
2 jalapenos, seeded
6 cloves garlic
1 cup sugar
1 cup rice vinegar
6 cups water
1 teaspoon paprika

**FOR THE MALT VINEGAR
    REDUCTION:**
½ cup sugar
4 cups malt vinegar

**FOR THE ROASTED GARLIC-
    CITRUS AIOLI:**
3 egg yolks
1 tablespoons Dijon mustard
4 cups canola oil
Juice of one orange, one lemon,
    and one lime
1½ teaspoons salt
3 tablespoons roasted garlic
½ cup water as needed

FOR THE STEAK FRIES:
4-6 russet potatoes
Oil
Salt and pepper

FOR THE SWORDFISH:
Swordfish, ¼ pound per person
Olive oil
Salt and pepper

To make the sweet chili sauce: Place all ingredients in a saucepan, and reduce to 4 cups. Then thicken with cornstarch slurry.

To make the malt vinegar reduction: Place the sugar and malt vinegar in a sauce pan and reduce to 1 cup.

To make the roasted garlic-citrus aioli: Place the egg yolks in a blender with the mustard and pulse for a few seconds. While the blender is running on low, slowly add the oil, citrus juice, salt, roasted garlic, and water as needed to create a smooth consistency.

To make the steak fries: Cut the potatoes into wedges and soak in water overnight. The next day, remove the potatoes from the water and pat dry. Fry in hot oil until golden brown. Remove excess oil, lightly salt, and bake 20 minutes in a 400°F oven.

To prepare the swordfish: Wash the swordfish steak. Pat dry, brush with olive oil, and sprinkle with salt and pepper. Place on a preheated grill; cook 5 minutes per side until desired doneness.

Hole In One
Bakery and Coffee Shop

During the summer months, the kayaks go on the car, a pot of fresh brewed coffee, two cups, and we are off to the lower Cape. Our first stop is for a doughnut from Hole in One. They specialize in fresh hand-cut doughnuts. I must admit—they are the best donuts on the Cape, bigger and moister than the rest.

I bought a few to take home and tested to see how long the freshness would hold up. I got to two days in the bag!

The Bazzano family bought the original Hole In One in 1989. "We use the best ingredients and the more expensive mixes to make our doughnuts," says Cindy Bazzano, 64, mother of four daughters. Cindy maintains there is nothing like a fresh hot doughnut made by hand. She is right!

Now the four daughters own and operate the business. On the busiest days during the summer months, Hole In One produces nearly 125 dozen hand-cut donuts daily in 20 different flavors. They have another location at 96 Route 6A, Orleans, MA 02653.

4295 Route 6A, North Eastham, MA 02642, (508) 255-9446

INDEX

ACKNOWLEDGEMENTS

I would like to thank several people who worked with me to produce this book. I could not have done this project without their help.

Thanks to my talented, creative photographer Francine Zaslow. Francine is primarily a studio photographer, and we go back several years. On countless commercial and editorial food shoots, I styled the food and she photographed it. This project took her from the comfort zone of her bright, sunny studio on an adventurous road trip. Often Deb Johnson, Francine's wonderfully efficient studio producer would join us or photo assistant Cody O'longhlin. Francine photographed the cover for the third edition of my book *Food Photography and Styling and we worked together on my latest, Great Italian American food in New England*. And my second photographer Manx Taiki Magyar who I met through a woman in the local farmer's market. Together we ran around the Cape shooting and checking out interesting places for all new material in this book.

Every writer needs a second pair of eyes, and a special thanks goes to my professional proofreader "food lover, creative cook" and long-time friend, Barton "Bart" Evans. We met at Modern Gourmet, Madeleine Kamman's cooking school in Newton MA.

I also want to thank my friend Paul Opacki and Donna DeFelice at Maypop Antiques for letting me use many of his unusual antiques for this book and other projects.

A special thanks to Amy Lyons, my editor for her commitment to me and my writing.

And, of course, this book would not be possible without the many chefs and owners of the restaurants, specialty shops, and eateries who generously opened their kitchens and shops to let me sample their recipes and food. Thank you.

PHOTO CREDITS

Photos by Francine Zaslow: x, xi, 7, 9, 11, 13, 15, 17, 19, 21, 25, 29, 31, 22, 34, 37, 38, 40, 47, 49, 51,66, 69, 73, 75, 77, 78, 79, 85, 91, 93, 94, 97, 99, 100, 102, 107, 108, 110, 118, 119, 120, 121, 122, 125, 127, 130, 133, 135, 136, 139, 145, 146, 147, 155, 157, 171, 189, 190, 191, 192, 194, 197, 201, 205, 206, 210, 213, 220, 221, 223, 231, 233, 242.

Photos by Manx Taiki Magyar: 2, 3, 5, 26, 27, 55, 57, 59, 60, 62, 63, 64, 65, 70, 80, 81, 87, 88, 111, 113, 117, 123, 132, 140, 142, 143, 151, 153, 158, 166, 167, 169, 172, 173, 175, 176, 179, 181, 183, 184, 186, 208, 209, 214, 215, 217, 224, 227, 228, 235.

Photos by John F. Carafoli: 22, 23, 53, 163, 241 (bottom)

Other photos: p. iv iStock.com/cindygoff; p. 43 Evgeny Karandaev/Shutterstock.com; p. 44 9to9studio/Shutterstock.com; pp. 82, 83 iStock.com/suefeldberg; p. 89 iStock.com/MSPhotographic; p. 150 Millbilly/Shutterstock.com; pp. 159, 160 courtesy of Clambakes, Etc...; p. 202 Deb Johnson; p. 219 EQRoy/Shutterstock.com; p. 241 (top) © Adam Detour.

ABOUT THE PHOTOGRAPHERS

Francine Zaslow has been creating beautiful images professionally for over two decades. After graduating from the University of the Arts in Philadelphia, she settled in Boston, where she built a diverse client base including Panera Bread, Fage, Au Bon Pain, Whole Foods, Fresh, Bose, Timberland, New Balance, and Mariposa.

Zaslow has won awards from *Communication Arts, Photo District News,* Big Picture Show, Saint Botolphs Society, and Hasselblad.

As an artist, Zaslow has always believed that inspiration comes from the unexpected. Reaching into the far corners of life's experiences, she has created a diverse collection of personal images.

Zaslow is both the photographer and the director, manipulating light, sculpting forms, and transforming her subjects with a deliberate eye.

You can view her photographs at francinezaslow.com.

Manx Taki Magyar was born in Yokohama, Japan, raised on Cape Cod, and graduated from Northeastern University in 2014 with a dual major in Cinema Studies/Communication and a minor in Video Production. He has worked in New York City and Boston on everything from reality TV to commercials to public access.

After graduating, Magyar spent a year traveling from Japan to Portugal—entirely without planes—while practicing his video and photography skills. He now works for Sandwich TV.

ABOUT THE AUTHOR

John F. Carafoli is an international food stylist, consultant, food writer and author of the seminal book *Food Photography and Styling*. He has also written two children's cookbooks, *Look Who's Cooking*, and *The Cookie Cookbook*. His is latest book is, *Great Italian American Food in New England, History, Traditions & Memories*. He has been published in *Gastronomica*, *The Journal of Food and Culture*, *The New York Times*, *The Boston Globe*, *L'italo-Americano Italian* newspaper, *Edible Cape Cod* (where he won an EDDY for Best use of Recipes in a feature) and has been profiled in the Italian publication of ER (*Emilia Romagna*). In addition to presenting papers at the Oxford Symposium on Food and Cookery in England, he has organized the biannual International Conference on Food Styling and Photography at Boston University. Carafoli was also featured on Food Network's Ultimate Kitchens and NPR. He also conducts culinary food, music and culture tours to Italy. Carafoli lives in West Barnstable, MA and can be found in the waters during the winter months gathering fresh oysters and clams.